SUPERGIRL

D1283642

BIZARROGIRL

SUPERGIRL

BIZARROGIRL

STERLING GATES
writer

JAMAL IGLE
JON SIBAL
BERNARD CHANG
MATT CAMP
MARCO RUDY
JOHN DELL
MARC DEERING
RICHARD FRIEND
ROBIN RIGGS
artists

NEI RUFFINO
JAMIE GRANT
JIM DEVLIN
BLOND
BRAD ANDERSON
colorists

JARED K. FLETCHER
TRAVIS LANHAM
STEVE WANDS
letterers

AMY REEDER,
RICHARD FRIEND
& GUY MAJOR
collection cover artists

SUPERGIRL based on characters created by **JERRY SIEGEL** and **JOE SHUSTER**
SUPERMAN created by **JERRY SIEGEL** and **JOE SHUSTER**
By special arrangement with the JERRY SIEGEL family

MATT IDELSON Editor – Original Series   WIL MOSS Associate Editor – Original Series   JEB WOODARD Group Editor – Collected Editions
STEVE COOK Design Director – Books   DAMIAN RYLAND Publication Design

BOB HARRAS Senior VP – Editor-in-Chief, DC Comics

DIANE NELSON President   ALISON GILL Senior VP – Manufacturing & Operations
DAN DIDIO and JIM LEE Co-Publishers   HANK KANALZ Senior VP – Editorial Strategy & Administration
GEOFF JOHNS Chief Creative Officer   JAY KOGAN VP – Legal Affairs
AMIT DESAI Senior VP – Marketing & Global Franchise Management   DEREK MADDALENA Senior VP – Sales & Business Development
NAIRI GARDINER Senior VP – Finance   JACK MAHAN VP – Business Affairs
SAM ADES VP – Digital Marketing   DAN MIRON VP – Sales Planning & Trade Development
BOBBIE CHASE VP – Talent Development   NICK NAPOLITANO VP – Manufacturing Administration
MARK CHIARELLO Senior VP – Art, Design & Collected Editions   CAROL ROEDER VP – Marketing
JOHN CUNNINGHAM VP – Content Strategy   EDDIE SCANNELL VP – Mass Account & Digital Sales
ANNE DEPIES VP – Strategy Planning & Reporting   COURTNEY SIMMONS Senior VP – Publicity & Communications
DON FALLETTI VP – Manufacturing Operations   JIM (SKI) SOKOLOWSKI VP – Comic Book Specialty & Newsstand Sales
LAWRENCE GANEM VP – Editorial Administration & Talent Relations   SANDY YI Senior VP – Global Franchise Management

SUPERGIRL: BIZARROGIRL

DC Comics, 2900 West Alameda Ave., Burbank, CA 91505
Printed by RR Donnelley, Salem, VA, USA. 8/5/16. First Printing.
ISBN: 978-1-4012-7012-4

Library of Congress Cataloging-in-Publication Data is available.

PEFC Certified

Printed on paper from
sustainably managed
forests and controlled
sources

PEFC/29-31-75   www.pefc.org

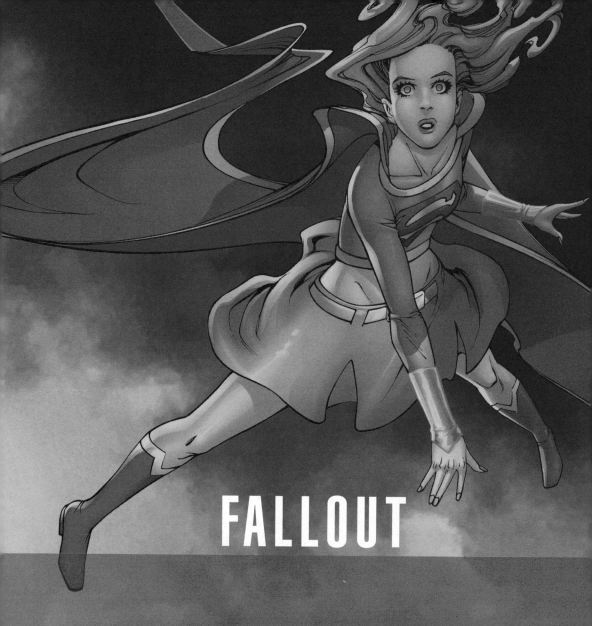

FALLOUT

JAMAL IGLE
penciller

JON SIBAL
inker

NEI RUFFINO
colorist

JARED K. FLETCHER
letterer

JAMAL IGLE & DAVID BARON
cover

WASHINGTON, D.C. THE PENTAGON.

PROJECT 7734. HALF A MILE BELOW.

NNNN!

WE'D DO IT ALL OVER AGAIN IF WE THOUGHT IT WOULD GET RID OF A *BRAT* LIKE *YOU*. I'M *SORRY* TO SEE YOU *SURVIVED* UNSCATHED.

HOW'D YOU PULL THAT OFF? USE SOMEONE ELSE AS A *KRYPTONIAN* SHIELD?

ENOUGH! YOU AND YOUR *FATHER* ARE *RESPONSIBLE* FOR THIS WAR--

TELL GENERAL *ZOD* THAT.

BETTER *YET,* TELL YOUR *MOTHER.* I *WATCHED* HER WHILE I WAS ON NEW KRYPTON. SHE WAS *FAR* FROM INNOCENT, SUPERGIRL.

AND AREN'T YOU FORGETTING SOMETHING? *YOU* KILLED *ME.* DESTROYED MY SUIT AND SENT MY CONSCIOUSNESS *ELSEWHERE.* IN FACT...

...LET ME *SHOW* YOU WHAT YOU DID TO ME.

W-WHAT? STOP!

...AND **RECOVERY** IS **STILL** FIRST AND **FOREMOST** ON PEOPLE'S MINDS.

ACROSS THE **PLANET,** THE JUSTICE LEAGUE HAS LED RECONSTRUCTION EFFORTS AT SITES HIT **HEAVIEST** BY THE KRYPTONIANS--

--INCLUDING CAIRO, PARIS, AND METROPOLIS.

METROPOLIS' OWN RESIDENT KRYPTONIAN, SUPERMAN, HAS BEEN CALLED BEFORE SEVERAL CONGRESSIONAL COMMITTEES TO DISCUSS THE DESTRUCTION OF NEW KRYPTON AND THE RESULTING WAR.

SINCE THE CONFLICT CEASED, THERE HAVE BEEN **ZERO** CONFIRMED KRYPTONIAN SIGHTINGS ON PLANET EARTH, SAVE FOR THE MAN OF STEEL.

NEXT ON WGBS, WRITER AND KRYPTONIAN EXPERT CATHERINE GRANT DISCUSSES HER UPCOMING BOOK, "SUPERGIRL: HOW A KRYPTONIAN UPSTART IS CORRUPTING TOMORROW'S YOUTH"--

LINDA'S ROOM
PLEASE KNOCK

WOW. WHAT HAPPENED?

SOME PEOPLE *TALK* IN THEIR SLEEP. OTHERS *WALK.*

I *HEAT-VISION,* APPARENTLY.

I'M SURE *SOMEONE* OUT THERE MAKES A SLEEP MASK THAT CAN HANDLE THAT.

NIGHTMARE?

YEAH.

...AGAIN.

CAN I MAKE YOU SOME EGGS?

NO.

TOAST?

NO.

COFFEE?

I HATE COFFEE.

OKAY. WELL. I'LL LEAVE YOU *ALONE,* THEN--

WAIT, LANA.

SORRY. I...I'M SORRY. I'M BEING A JERK. A SLEEP-DEPRIVED *JERK.* I JUST WANTED TO SAY...

THANK YOU. FOR LETTING ME MOVE BACK IN. YOU *DIDN'T* HAVE TO DO THAT, ESPECIALLY... ESPECIALLY AFTER THE WAY I TREATED YOU.

SO... THANKS.

YOU'RE *WELCOME,* KARA. AND YOU'RE ALWAYS WELCOME HERE. FAR AS I'M CONCERNED, YOU'RE FAMILY--

YEAH. ABOUT *THAT...*THIS MIGHT BE *WEIRD,* BUT CAN I ASK YOU FOR A FAVOR?

I MEAN, MORE THAN A FAVOR. IT'S SORT OF A...

...A *LIFE CHANGE.* CAN WE SIT DOWN?

DO YOU REMEMBER WHEN I TOLD YOU TO CALL ME LINDA?

YES?

I, UM...I WAS THINKING I WANT TO MAKE THAT...WELL, *PERMANENT.*

...WHAT?

I WANT TO QUIT USING MY KRYPTONIAN NAME *ENTIRELY.*

BECOME LINDA LANG FULL-TIME.

ARE YOU...ARE YOU *SURE* YOU WANT TO *DO* THAT, KARA? I MEAN, YOUR NAME IS *IMPORTANT*, IT'S WHO YOU *ARE*--

I'VE BEEN THINKING ABOUT THIS A *LOT*.

READING ABOUT IMMIGRANTS WHO TOOK ON NEW NAMES TO HELP THEM FIT IN WHEN THEY MOVED TO NEW PLACES.

I'VE GOT TO...WELL, METROPOLIS IS MY *HOME* NOW. SO IT'S IMPORTANT THAT I *ACCEPT* THAT. *LIVE* THAT.

BUT, KARA, WON'T YOU BE LOSING PART OF WHAT MADE YOU *KRYPTONIAN?* REJECTING YOUR PEOPLE--

MY PEOPLE ARE *GONE*, LANA. *ALL* OF THEM. MOM. DAD. THARA. EVEN POOR ZAL-TEL.

ME AND KAL ARE THE ONLY ONES WHO...

LOOK, ALL "KARA ZOR-EL" IS GOING TO DO IS REMIND ME OF EVERYTHING I'VE *LOST*. I'D RATHER THINK ABOUT THE *FUTURE* INSTEAD.

THE LANGS WOULD BE *HONORED* TO HAVE YOU FULL-TIME, LINDA. AND FORGET ABOUT WHAT HAPPENED BEFORE. IT'S OLD HISTORY.

FAMILY *FORGIVES* TEENAGERS.

THANK YOU.

HAVE YOU... HAVE YOU THOUGHT ABOUT WHAT *SUPERGIRL'S* GOING TO DO, THEN--

YEAH. JUST LIKE KARA ZOR-EL, SUPERGIRL'S *GOING AWAY*, TOO.

FOR *GOOD*.

DON'T LIKE WHAT, MR. DELGADO?

THIS. KEEPING SUPERWOMAN HERE. SHE'S A SECURITY RISK, DR. HOSHI, AND--

RIGHT...NOT MY BUSINESS, THEN, BUT HOW'S... WHATEVER YOU'RE DOING COMING ALONG?

AND SHE'S A PATIENT OF MINE.

YOU'RE HEAD OF SECURITY. YOUR MEN HAVE MADE SURE SHE'S NOT A SECURITY RISK.

YOU SIGNED THE CONFIDENTIALITY AGREEMENT EVERY-ONE ELSE SIGNS, GANGBUSTER. ANYTHING THAT HAPPENS AT S.T.A.R. IS YOUR BUSINESS.

SUPERWOMAN WAS INFUSED WITH SEVERAL STRAINS OF ALIEN D.N.A. USING A COMBINATION OF SCIENCE AND MAGIC, GIVING HER EXTRATERRESTRIAL ABILITIES.

WE'RE USING THE DEVICE SUPERGIRL AND I DESIGNED FOR COMBATING THE INSECT QUEEN TO FILTER SUPERWOMAN'S D.N.A. AND RESTORE HER HUMANITY.

LOOKS PAINFUL.

WE'RE COMBING THROUGH EVERY CELL IN HER BODY, ONE BY ONE. IT'S NOT A PRETTY SCIENCE...

AAAAAAAAH!

CAN YOU CURE HER?

WHATEVER GENERAL LANE DID TO HER, HE DIDN'T MEAN FOR IT TO BE PERMANENT. WE'VE MADE STRIDES, BUT--

"...NOR IS IT, UNFORTUNATELY, PAINLESS."

CHRISTAL'S CAFE, CORNER OF BINDER AND PAPP.

"I DON'T WANT TO *PRY*, LINDA, BUT..."

...WHERE DID YOU GO?

WHAT?

WELL, YOU WERE GONE FOR *SIX WEEKS*. I WAS WORRIED WHEN WE DIDN'T *HEAR* FROM YOU AFTER ALL... OF EVERYTHING, SO I JUST WAS WONDERING--

LANA, IT...IT DOESN'T *MATTER*. CAN WE CHANGE THE SUBJECT, PLEASE?

OKAY. WELL THEN, LINDA LANG, WHERE DO YOU GO FROM HERE? DO YOU HAVE SOMETHING IN *MIND*?

I--I GUESS I DON'T REALLY *KNOW* YET.

WHY?

I'VE BEEN *THINKING* ABOUT THIS. CAN I MAKE A SUGGESTION...?

OHHH-KAYYY...

WE *ALL* HIT POINTS IN OUR LIFE WHERE WE'RE *UNSURE* ABOUT WHAT TO DO NEXT. I HAD ONE WHEN I WAS ROUGHLY YOUR AGE.

ONE THING THAT HELPED ME WAS *COLLEGE*. HAVE YOU THOUGHT ABOUT ATTENDING METROPOLIS UNIV--

23

THOOM

WHAT WAS THAT?!

I DON'T KNOW.

≶ZZZAT≶ REPORTS COMING IN!

≶FZZAAAT≶ HUGE SHOCK WAVE TEARING THROUGH THE CITY ≶KKZZAT≶ SHATTERING WINDOWS--

--RESULT OF ≶ZZT≶ CRASH AT CENTENNIAL PARK! MEMBERS OF THE JUSTICE LEAGUE HAVE BEEN SPOTTED EN ROUTE--

"HELL..."

...I MIGHT BE OUTTA MY *LEAGUE* HERE, DOC.

NONSENSE. I'VE SEEN YOU IN *COMBAT.*

SHOOTING GIANT BUGS IN THE *FACE* AIN'T QUITE THE SAME AS *THIS.*

"C'MON, LANA..."

...I'M GONNA TAKE YOU TO MET-GEN TO GET THESE CUTS STITCHED.

WHAT... WHAT DID THE NEWS--

SOMETHING JUST *CRASHED* IN CENTENNIAL PARK...

"...SOMETHING *BIG.*"

THIS IS JUST...*WEIRD.* THERE WAS AN *EXPLOSION,* RIGHT? BIG BOOM BEFORE WE GOT HERE?

SO WHY IS EVERYTHING *FROZEN?*

YOU'RE A S.T.A.R. LABS EMPLOYEE NOW, MR. DELGADO.

GET *USED* TO WEIRD.

"YOU'RE NOT GOING *DOWN* THERE?"

THE JUSTICE LEAGUE'S SUPPOSEDLY ON-SCENE ALREADY. SO IT'S NOT MY PROBLEM.

NO...NO, I SAW THE JUSTICE LEAGUE, THEY'RE IN CAIRO--

YOU'RE TELLING ME YOU'RE NOT EVEN GOING TO GO LOOK? AT ALL?

YEAH, WELL. SOME OF THEM MUST NOT BE.

"WHAT IF SOMEONE NEEDS YOUR HELP?"

HUH. WHERE'VE WE SEEN THIS STUFF BEFORE?

CRYSTAL TECHNOLOGY. LOOKS KRYPTONIAN. REFUGEES FROM NEW KRYPTON, OR...?

"WHAT IF SOMEONE'S HURT?"

LOOK AROUND, KARA. PEOPLE OUT THERE NEED YOU. YOU CAN USE YOUR GIFTS TO--

"GIFTS"? THESE "GIFTS" MAKE ME A TARGET, LANA. THEY MAKE ME DANGEROUS TO EVERYONE AROUND ME.

AND AS YOU'LL RECALL, THE LAST TIME I TRIED TO HELP SOMEONE, I GOT A PLANET FULL OF MY PEOPLE BLOWN UP--

"...AND THEN SUPERGIRL COULDN'T SAVE ANY OF THEM."

I WOULDN'T GET TOO CLOSE, DOC. COULD BE BOOBY-TRAPPED, OR--

THAT WASN'T YOUR FAULT AND YOU KNOW IT--

IT DOESN'T MATTER WHOSE FAULT YOU THINK IT WAS, LANA! 80,000 PEOPLE WERE PUT IN DANGER BECAUSE OF SOMETHING I DID...

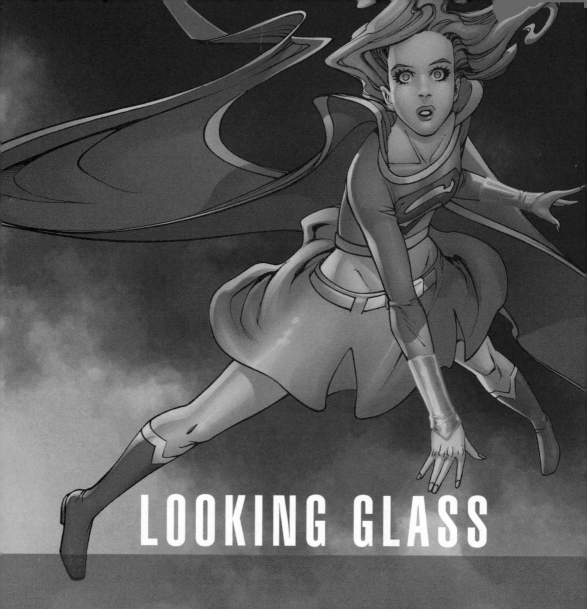

LOOKING GLASS

JAMAL IGLE
penciller

JON SIBAL
inker

JAMIE GRANT
colorist

JARED K. FLETCHER
letterer

SHANE DAVIS & JAMIE GRANT
cover

THAT WAS *AWESOME!*

COOL MOTORCYCLE!

GOOD. STAY FAR AWAY FROM WHATEVER'S HAPPENING AND KEEP YOUR HEAD DOWN.

THANKS. MY GIRLFRIEND HELPED ME FIX IT UP.

YOU'VE GOT A *GIRLFRIEND,* TOO? COOL!

YEAH. SHE'S PRETTY GREAT.

NOW STAY AWAY FROM DANGER AND TRY TO FIND A POLICE OFFICER IF YOU CAN. OR A SUPER-HERO.

WAIT, SO YOU'RE *NOT* A POLICEMAN?

WHO *ARE* YOU THEN?! AND WHERE ARE YOU *GOING?*

VRRMMMM

JIMMY OLSEN! AND I'M GONNA GET *CLOSER* TO WHATEVER'S MESSING UP DOWNTOWN.

WHAT?! *WHY?*

SO I CAN TAKE A PICTURE OF IT.

COOL.

JIMMY OLSEN IS COOL.

OKAY, SO. A **SOMETHING** IS TEARING UP METROPOLIS.

TYPICAL WEDNESDAY FOR US, REALLY...

GOOD GOD. WHATEVER'S DOWN FIFTH, IT MUST BE DOING SOME REAL DAMAGE TO CAUSE A PANIC LIKE THIS.

--SOMEONE **HELP** US--

--SHE LOOKED AT MY ARM AND NOW I CAN'T **MOVE** IT--

--THINK I'M BLEEDING. CAN SOMEONE TELL ME IF I'M BLEEDING? I CAN'T **SEE** ANYTHING--

DOOMSDAY-LEVEL DAMAGE.

I SHOULDN'T'VE LEFT THE 70-200MM AT HOME. I WOULDN'T NEED TO GET SO CLOSE TO THIS TO SHOOT.

STILL, BEATS GETTING THE CHIEF COFFEE.

HOPEFULLY THIS DUST WILL CLEAR OUT ENOUGH THAT I CAN--

HOLY--

37

I NEED EYEWITNESS ACCOUNTS, PEOPLE!
I WANT EVERY VIDEO OF IT THAT'S ON YOUTUBE RIGHT NOW EMBEDDED TO THE DAILY PLANET WEBSITE!
AND WHERE'S OLSEN? I NEEDED A CUP OF COFFEE TWENTY MINUTES AGO--
MR. WHITE?
IMAGES FROM JIMMY'S CAMERA JUST HIT THE SERVER.
HE'S DOWN THERE? GOOD! I WANT TO PAY THAT KID FOR SOMETHING WORTHWHILE FOR ONCE--
SIR, HE'S MORE THAN DOWN THERE. LOOK.
PERRY, I NEED TO TALK TO YOU--
NOT NOW, LANG. WHAT AM I LOOKING AT, NORRIS?
KORD
IT'S NORRIE, SIR. AND THESE ARE PICTURES THAT JIMMY'S CAMERA AUTO-UPLOADED TO THE SYSTEM. WHATEVER'S DOWN THERE...
...GUESS IT WASN'T READY FOR A CLOSE-UP.
JIMMY...
GREAT CAESAR'S GHOST.

SOMEBODY CALL THE SCIENCE POLICE! OLSEN'S BEEN KIDNAPPED AGAIN!

SCIENCE POLICE ARE STILL REBUILDING, SIR.

THEN CALL THE S.C.U.! AND WHY DID LANE PICK TODAY TO GO TO PHILADELPHIA AND COVER THAT SUPERMAN THING!?

NORRIE, CAN YOU ENHANCE THESE PICTURES AT ALL?

SURE, MS. LANG. EASY.

THERE. CAN YOU BLOW THAT UP AND FILTER THE IMAGE? OR AT LEAST GIVE ME AN IDEA WHAT THAT IS?

THE DUST AND NOISE IN THE IMAGE IS PRETTY BAD, BUT I CAN TRY.

HEY!

S.T.A.R. LABS JANITOR ON THE PHONE, PERRY! HE SAYS A SPACESHIP CRASHED THROUGH THEIR OFFICES ABOUT TWENTY MINUTES AGO!

A SPACESHIP?

VOILÀ!

OH MY GOD.

YOU'RE AN UNPAID INTERN, RIGHT, NORRIE? WITH AN OPTION TO HIRE ON?

UM. YES, MA'AM?

GREAT. I'M HIRING YOU FOR THE BUSINESS SECTION.

YOU'LL REPORT TO ME TOMORROW MORNING ONCE I CLEAR IT WITH H.R.-- AND EMAIL ME THAT JPEG RIGHT NOW.

Y-YES, MA'AM!

VZZZ VZZZ VZZZ

LANA LANG
incoming call

LEXTEL

HELLO?

WHERE **ARE** YOU RIGHT NOW?

I'M AT THE HOUSE. WHY?

BECAUSE A **BIZARRO** WITH YOUR FACE IS **TEARING** UP THE FINANCIAL DISTRICT!

WHAT?!?

YEAH. SO, WAY I SEE IT, YOU'VE GOT **TWO** OPTIONS.

ONE, YOU CAN CONTINUE TO **WALLOW** IN SELF-PITY OVER THE FACT THAT YOU COULDN'T SAVE NEW KRYPTON FROM A POWER-STEALING, WORLD-SHATTERING BLAST.

OR **TWO**, YOU COULD GET OUT OF **BED** AND GO SAVE WHOEVER YOU **CAN**.

YOUR CHOICE, **KARA**, BUT YOU MIGHT ASK YOURSELF, WHAT WOULD YOUR **PEOPLE** WANT YOU TO DO?

...IT'S LINDA.

IF YOU'RE GOING TO KEEP **PRETENDING** YOU DON'T CARE ABOUT **PEOPLE**, NO, IT'S **NOT**.

WE'RE SUPPOSED TO BE FIGHTERS, NOT SIT-AROUND-AND-MOPE-ERS. NOW...

OKAY...

KID, WAKE UP.

KID!

OLSEN, RISE AND SHINE!

WELCOME BACK. YOU JUST WOKE UP TO A NIGHTMARE.

GANGBUSTER? WHAT--

SHHHHH! SHE'LL *HEAR* YOU. AND TRUST ME, YOU *DON'T* WANT HER TO.

WHY *NOT?*

≥NNNGH≤ WHERE...?

GUY OVER THERE TRIED TO SHOUT FOR *HELP.*

SHE CAME BACK AND SHUT HIM UP.

PERMANENTLY.

BUT WHAT DOES SHE *WANT* FROM US? WHY ARE *WE*--

--MMMMPH!

SHHHH.

NEWS SAID THERE WAS AN EXPLOSION AT CENTENNIAL PARK, AND FIFTH AND GLENMORGAN'S THREE BLOCKS EAST. SO I'VE GOT A PLACE TO *START* LOOKING...

HEY! DOWN *HERE!* HEEEY!

'SCUSE ME, SON. ARE YOU LOOKING FOR YOUR *PARENTS?*

UM, Y-YEAH? YOU'RE A *COP?*

WHAT'S YOUR *NAME?*

E-ELI BROWN. SIR.

OH, CALLING ME SIR. THAT'S *GOOD.* GOOD MANNERS, SON.

COME WITH ME, ELI BROWN. WE'RE COLLECTING ALL OF THE KIDS IN THE AREA WHO MIGHT'VE BEEN SEPARATED FROM THEIR PARENTS. MAKES IT EASIER FOR THEM TO BE *FOUND.*

WAS... WAS THAT DOOR THERE A SECOND AGO?

'COURSE IT WAS. NOW LET'S HURRY ALONG...

...WE WANT YOU TO BE HOME BEFORE *DINNER.*

"LET *GO* OF HIM!"

45

NO, OH, YOU NOT!

KRRREEK

THE HECK'S HAPPENING, OLSEN?!

I...I DON'T *KNOW.*

YOU'RE SUPERMAN'S PAL! AREN'T YOU SUPPOSED TO BE THE *EXPERT,* KID?

THAT MEANS IF KRYPTONIANS HAVE A KIND OF VISION THAT LETS THEM SEE COMPLETELY *THROUGH* THINGS...THEN THAT MEANS...

YEAH?

...THAT *MEANS...*

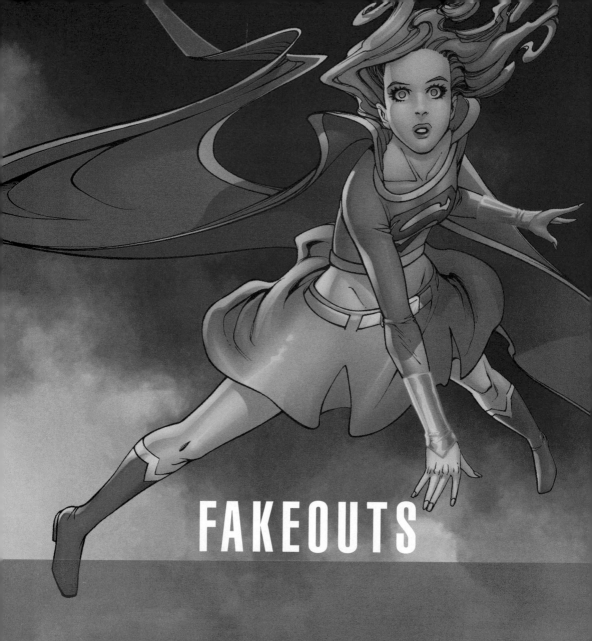

FAKEOUTS

JAMAL IGLE
penciller

JOHN DELL, MARC DEERING & RICHARD FRIEND
inkers

JAMIE GRANT & JIM DEVLIN
colorists

JARED K. FLETCHER
letterer

AMY REEDER, RICHARD FRIEND & GUY MAJOR
cover

BIZARRO WORLD.

THE ANTI-ARCTIC.

SIX WEEKS AGO.

"BIZARRRROOOO! ME NEED YOU!"

RUMMBLLLLLL

HALL OF SCIENCE

INTERGALTIC GOO

BIZARRO #1! METROPLIS AM GONE NOW! UN-CENTRAL CITY AM MORE WRECKED, TOO! DESTRUCTION EVEN COME HERE, TO FORTRESS OF TOGETHERNESS!

ME AM SAD TO BE HERE AND NOT THERE! ME WANT TO DRAW PICTURES OF DESTROYED CITIES!

YOU AM GREATEST HERO OF BIZARRO WORLD, BIZARRO #1, AND NOW AM TIME TO SHINE! WHERE ARE YOU?!

BIZARRO #1...WHAT...

...WHAT AM YOU DOING?

61

BUT--BUT *HOW?* SHE--

SHE WAS *TRAPPING* ME. *ENCASING* ME WITH HER *"SOLID-VISION."*

"THE FLASH *TRAINED* ME TO HANDLE THAT KINDA THING."

MR. FREEZE, CAPTAIN COLD, MINISTER BLIZZARD-- ALL OF THEM WILL TRY TO *FREEZE* YOU DEAD IN YOUR TRACKS, COAT YOU IN *ICE.*

YOU GOTTA KNOW HOW TO *COUNTER.* IF YOU VIBRATE AT *SUPERSPEED*, YOUR MOLECULES WILL BE ABLE TO SLIP *BETWEEN* THE MOLECULES OF WHATEVER'S FREEZING YOU.

I DON'T KNOW IF I'M THAT *FAST.*

I'VE SEEN YOUR COUSIN RUN BEFORE, KARA. IF THE SITUATION'S DIRE ENOUGH THAT YOU GET THAT KRYPTONIAN *ADRENALINE* PUMPING THROUGH YOU?

"TRUST ME, YOU'LL BE *MORE* THAN FAST ENOUGH."

OKAY...SO NOW WHAT'S THE PLAN?

LET'S GET THESE PEOPLE OUT OF HERE FIRST. THEN, I'M GOING TO NEED DR. LIGHT'S HELP WITH *UNCONSCIOUS-GIRL* OVER THERE--

BOOM!

WORD EDIT FILE VIEW INSERT FONT TABLE WINDOW HELP

DOES SUPERGIRL HAVE A DAILY PLANET INFORMANT?

By Cat Grant

--ABSOLUTELY *NOT*, LOIS!

CLARK *ASKED* FOR THE SUPERMAN STORY, SO I *GAVE* IT TO HIM. I WANT YOU BACK HERE A.S.A.P. TO COVER WHATEVER'S WRECKING THE *CITY*--

PERRY! I'VE GOT A *BEAUTIFUL* STORY FOR YOU ABOUT SUPERGIR--

MM-HM... UH-HUH.... RIGHT...

PERRY, I--

D. McKINN

BLOOD, POLICE, OR FLAMES, CAT? AND IT'D BETTER BE *ALL* OF THE ABOVE!

I-I'VE GOT A STORY THAT'S TOMORROW'S FRONT PAGE--

SUPERMAN'S TOMORROW'S FRONT PAGE. SO YOU CAN WAIT UNTIL I'M OFF THE PHONE. AM I CLEAR?

LOIS, EMAIL THAT ARTICLE AND *GET. ON. A. PLANE.* NO EXCUSES. *AT ALL!*

MS. GRANT?

WHAT'S ALL *THAT*?

YOUR *MAIL.*

YOUR *BOOK PUBLISHER* DECIDED TO *FORWARD* THE PLANET ALL YOUR *FAN MAIL*--

YES, YES, GREAT. LEAVE THE CART NEXT TO MY DESK.

PERRY, HOLD ON A SECOND! THIS IS *IMPORTANT!*

THIS CITY DOESN'T *STOP* BECAUS[E] SUPERMAN'S [I]N TOWN, LOIS[!] NOW GET *BAC[K]* HERE!

OH.

NOT ANOTHER ONE.

EXCUSE ME?

THE GRANT PLANET[...] [...]IC WAY

UH, NOTHING. EXCUSE *ME,* I NEED TO GO--

CAT!

WHAT DID YOU WANT?

UM. NOTHING, PERRY. I'VE, UH, I'VE GOT TO *RUN.* APPOINTMENT I FORGOT ABOUT!

TA TA!

...HMPH. THESE REPORTERS ARE GONNA BE THE DEATH OF ME.

CHOW CHOW CHOW CHOW

ME AM *TICKLISH*, BUT YOU NOT HITTING RIGHT SPOTS.

YOU GOT FREE AND TRIED TO POOP ON MY PARTY, SO ME RENAME YOU *PARTYPOOPER*, GANGBUSTER!

YEAH, WELL, NOT EVERYONE CAN HANDLE BEING SET ON *FIRE*. I WAS TRYING TO GIVE THOSE PEOPLE A *CHANCE*--

SHHRAK

AAAHH!!

NNGG--!

NOW ME MUST FIND GUESTS AGAIN AND HAND OUT PARTY FAVORS.

BUT FIRST...

BOOM.

WHEEEEEEEEE!

YOU OKAY?

THINK... SO.

TRIED TO...GET HER *AWAY* FROM EVERYBODY...TURNS OUT SHE'S NOT VULNERABLE...TO *BULLETS*...

MM. SHE BROKE TWO OF YOUR METACARPALS. YOUR SKULL LOOKS FINE, THOUGH.

YEAH, WELL...I'M A HARDHEADED GUY.

APPARENTLY. THINK YOU CAN FIND YOUR WAY TO METROPOLIS GENERAL?

SURE. WHERE'RE *YOU* GOING?

I'VE GOT AN APPOINTMENT WITH A DIFFERENT DOCTOR.

LA LA LA LA! YOU SO UGLY!

YOU AM UGLY FLOOOOWEEEERS--

SHNNNNG

HOW DO *YOU* LIKE BEING *FROZEN,* YOU BIZARRO#$%#--

KRRSHHH

YOU AM GOOD FRIEND, BIZARRO ME! YOU COME TO PLAY WITH BIZARROGIRL!

I'M NOT YOUR *FRIEND,* BIZARROGIRL.

IN FACT, I THINK I'M YOUR *ENEMY.*

THAT AM *UN-FALSE.* YOU FIND ME IN METROPOLIS AND OUT OF TOWN. FRIENDS *FIND* FRIENDS, ESPECIALLY AFTER GREAT TRAGEDY!

GREAT *TRAGEDY? WHAT?*

BIZARRO SENT ME TO EARTH AS *REFUGEE.* SAVE ME FROM GODSHIP!

A LINE FROM AN OLD SCI-FI MOVIE?

IT TAKES TIME TO BUILD UP A BEAM THAT *STRONG*, BUT IT HELPS I'M STILL REALLY, REALLY TICKED OFF AT BEING KNOCKED OUT.

SO, SHE'S DEFEATED. WHAT NOW?

OLD? I *JUST* SAW IT. I *WAS* FLYING THROUGH *SPACE* WHEN IT CAME OUT, YOU KNOW.

NICE ORBITAL LASER, BY THE WAY.

WHAT? OH.

BIZARRO HAS BEEN MAKING CLONES OF *HIMSELF* USING A SPECIAL TYPE OF, UH, "CLONE VISION." HE DERIVES THE POWER UNDER BLUE SUNLIGHT. KAL FOUND THAT OUT.

FASCINATING. AND WHY IS SHE DRESSED LIKE YOU?

BIZARRO MADE A *PLANET* FOR HIMSELF, THEN PEOPLED IT ENTIRELY WITH BIZARROS GROWN FROM HIM.*

*AS SEEN IN *SUPERMAN: ESCAPE FROM BIZARRO WORLD!* --BIZARRO MATT

BIZARRO CREATED A *PLANET* HE BECOMES QUITE POWERFU UNDER A BLUE SUN, THEN.

AND DID I HEAR HER SAY SOMETHING OVER THE COMM ABOUT BEING A *REFUGEE*?

WAIT, WHAT ARE YOU DOING?

I TOLD YOU, SHE'S GOING BACK TO S.T.A.R. LABS. WE CAN'T LET A DANGEROUS *EXTRATERRESTRIAL* GO *UNCHECKED*--

YOU MEAN LIKE ME?

I'LL TAKE HER BACK TO S.T.A.R. LABS AND *IMPRISON* HER. I'M VERY *CURIOUS* TO KNOW WHAT MAKES HER WORK.

THE FIRST BIZARRO WAS A CLONE OF SUPERMAN. HOW ARE THERE *MORE* OF THEM?

...SUPERGIRL?

NO. *YOU*, I TRUST. *SHE'S* A *MURDERER*, SUPERGIRL. SHE KILLED THAT MAN BACK IN THE TUNNEL, AND LORD KNOWS HOW MANY OTHER INNOCENTS.

...YEAH. I KNOW.

DR. LIGHT, I THINK YOU'RE GOING TO BE *REALLY* MAD AT ME LATER. AND I'M REALLY *SORRY*.

"SORRY"? WHAT FOR--

HEY! SUPERGIRL! CAN I GET A--

--QUICK... PICTURE...?

WHAT'RE YOU DOING, SUPERGIRL?

FWOOO

HEY!

KMMMM
KMMMM

SORRY, JIMMY.

SKOOOOM

HEY, ARE YOU OKAY?!

I'M FINE.

WAS THAT *SUPERGIRL* IN THERE? WHERE'S SHE GOING?!

I...I...

"...I DON'T *KNOW.*"

COORDINATES AM SET. DESTINATION: BIZARRO WORLD.

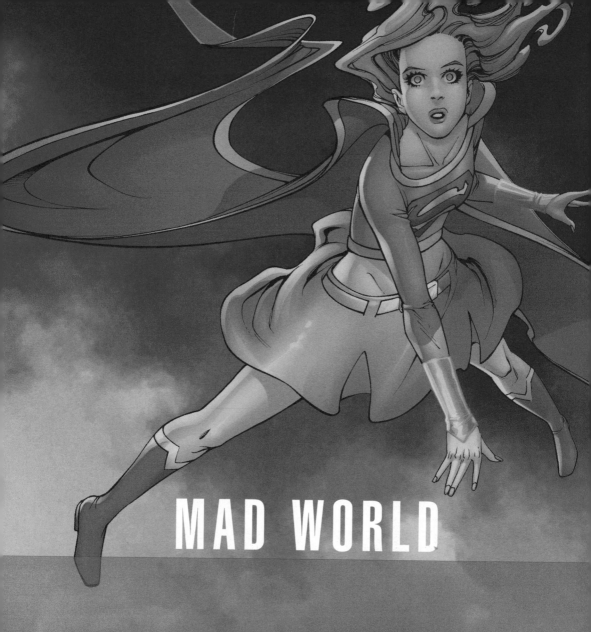

MAD WORLD

JAMAL IGLE
penciller

JON SIBAL
inker

BLOND
colorist

TRAVIS LANHAM
letterer

AMY REEDER, RICHARD FRIEND & GUY MAJOR
cover

...WHAT AM I LOOKING AT?

THAT AM THE GODSHIP.

IT CAME FROM SPACE, SLAMMING DOWN INTO PLANET WHERE IT SAT FOR DAYS. BUT THEN...

"...I MIGHT'VE MADE IT MAD..."

YOU AM LEGAL ALIENS! YOU AM NOT ALLOWED ON BIZARRO WORLD!

"...AND IT SENT THINGS AFTER ME.

FOR ALL HER **PERFECTIONS,** ME **HATE** HER, SO ME DECIDE TO TAKE HER TO EARTH AND LIVE WITH PUBLIC IDENTITIES.

LET GODSHIP **EAT** BIZARRO WORLD.

THESE AM BITTER AND HARD!

THAT THING IS ON THE OTHER SIDE OF THE **WORLD,** RIGHT?

WHAT AM YOU PLANNING?

YOU TWO STAY HERE. I WANT TO KNOW **MORE** ABOUT THESE ALIENS, AND I WANT TO SEE WHAT'S INSIDE THAT **SHIP.**

THAT AM BAD IDEA, SUPERGIRL.

THIS IS BIZARRO WORLD. ALL OF MY **BAD** IDEAS ARE **GOOD** ONES HERE, RIGHT?

DON'T WORRY. I'LL BE **FINE.**

THAT... THAT AM NOT **EXACTLY** HOW BIZARRO WORLD WORKS.

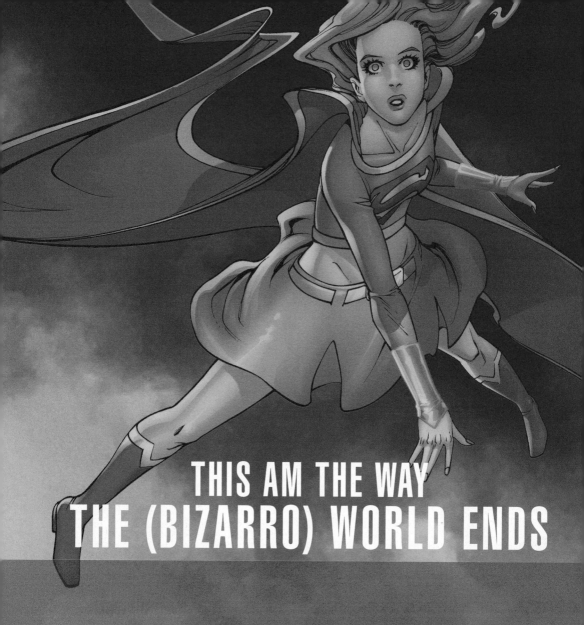

THIS AM THE WAY
THE (BIZARRO) WORLD ENDS

BERNARD CHANG
artist

BLOND
colorist

TRAVIS LANHAM
letterer

AMY REEDER, RICHARD FRIEND & GUY MAJOR
cover

AAIIEEEE--

"EVERYONE ON THIS PLANET IS GOING TO *DIE*."

THAT MONSTER-- WHATEVER IT *IS*--IS CHIPPING AWAY AT YOUR PLANET, AND PRETTY SOON THE CORE WILL DESTABILIZE.

WHAT WILL DESTABILIZING THE CORE OF BIZARRO WORLD DO?

YOU SAW WHAT HAPPENED TO THE BOTTOM HALF OF BIZARRO WORLD?

NO. ER, YES?

THAT WAS *NOTHING* COMPARED TO WHAT *WILL* HAPPEN IF WE DON'T GET IT AWAY FROM BIZARRO WORLD.

SO WHAT AM YOUR *PLAN*, SUPERGIRL?

BY ABSORBING BLUE SUNLIGHT, YOU GAIN THE ABILITY TO MAKE *CLONES* OF YOURSELF, RIGHT, BIZARRO? "BIZARRO VISION."

ER... YES?

WHEN SUPERMAN WAS HERE, HE DEVELOPED NEW POWERS AFTER BEING UNDER THE BLUE SUN. "SUPER VISION."

I'M GOING TO ACCELERATE THAT PROCESS IN ME AND TRY A LITTLE EXPERIMENT ON ALL OF US.

WHAT IF THIS DOESN'T WORK?

THEN I'LL HAVE FAILED AN ENTIRE RACE FOR A SECOND TIME.

...BUT ONLY THE FIRST FEW SECONDS.

NO!

AAAHH!

EVEN MAKING SUPER CLONES FROM BIZARRO...

...THEY'RE STILL NOT POWERFUL ENOUGH TO WIN THIS FIGHT.

I NEED *ALL* SCIENCE AND MILITARY GUILD MEMBERS TO FOLLOW ME!

WATCH YOUR *FLANKS*, PEOPLE!

AND STAY *CLEAR* OF THE MAIN BODY'S LINE OF *SIGHT!*

FOR THE FIRST FEW SECONDS, IT SEEMS LIKE WE MIGHT HAVE A SHOT AT WINNING THIS...

BIZARRO #1! ME--ME--

ME AM UN-BRAVE, BUT ME NOT WANT TO *DIE!*

BIZARROGIRL, COME BACK! THIS AM WAR!

COME BACK!

"...WHERE'S BIZARROGIRL?"

STUPID MACHINE! WHY AM YOU NOT SIMPLER!?

BIZARRO BIZARRO ME HAD NO TROUBLE MAKING YOU WORK--

SKRRAAZT

AHHH!

RRRRR! ME AM SMART!

WHY CAN ME NOT MAKE ANYTHING WORK!?!

WHY AM ME NOT BRAVE ENOUGH TO STAY AND FIGHT?!

RR. RR. RR.

BUT A FEW MONTHS AGO, I MADE A DECISION.

"NEVER AGAIN WOULD I LET SOME *IDIOT* COMMIT GENOCIDE.

NEVER AGAIN WOULD I LET SOMEONE TAKE ADVANTAGE OF PEOPLE WHO CAN'T DEFEND THEMSELVES.

AND THAT'S WHAT THAT...*THING* IS DOING. TAKING ADVANTAGE OF YOUR *PEOPLE*.

SO IT'S UP TO *US* TO STOP IT BEFORE IT DRIVES YOUR RACE TO *EXTINCTION*.

BUT BIZARRO BIZARRO ME...

...ME AM NOT *WORRIED* ABOUT EXTINCTION OF RACE.

"ME AM ONLY WORRIED ABOUT ME AND *COUSIN*.

"AM THAT *SELFISH*?"

...NO. NO, IT'S NOT SELFISH AT *ALL*, BIZARROGIRL.

BUT IF WE DON'T GET OUT THERE SOON, A LOT OF OTHER PEOPLE'S LOVED ONES ARE GOING TO DIE, TOO. YOU UNDERSTAND?

YOU AM RIGHT...IT'S JUST...I...

...H-HOW DID YOU GET TO BE SO *BRAVE* WHEN ME SO *COWARDLY*, BIZARRO BIZARRO ME?

I'M A BIZARRO *YOU*, REMEMBER? I FEEL THE *OPPOSITE* OF WHATEVER YOU'RE FEELING.

TELL YOU WHAT: I'LL *TRADE* YOU FEELINGS. IF I LET MYSELF BE *SCARED*...

...WILL YOU BE *BRAVE* FOR YOUR WORLD?

AFTER TRYING FOR **DAYS**, I FINALLY GOT THROUGH TO THE **GREEN LANTERN CORPS**.

THEY COLLECTED THE GODSHIP, AND TOLD ME IT WAS A TYPE OF WORLD-EATER CALLED AN **ASH'KA'PHAGEOUS**.

..."GODSHIP" IS **WAY** EASIER TO PRONOUNCE.

IN THE DAYS FOLLOWING THE CREATURE'S DEFEAT, AS I TRIED TO PUT THE BIZARRO ROCKET BACK TOGETHER, BIZARROGIRL WENT **MISSING**.

WE SEARCHED BIZARRO WORLD OVER, AND FINALLY FOUND HER IN A SMALL CAVE ON THE EASTERN SEABOARD.

BIZARROGIRL? WHAT ARE YOU DOING?

SAD HARBOR ROAD EYE-LAND

ME **SAVED** BIZARRO WORLD, SUPERGIRL...

...SO WHY DO ME **NOW** HURT INSIDE?

...OKAY. LET'S TALK ABOUT IT.

AND SO WE TALKED. ONCE THE CRISIS WAS OVER, SHE'D STARTED **THINKING** ABOUT HER ACTIONS. ABOUT WHAT SHE'D DONE ON EARTH.

IT WAS LIKE LISTENING TO A CHILD DISCOVER THAT WHAT THEY DO ACTUALLY HAS **CONSEQUENCES**.

BECAUSE OF WHAT WE'D DONE, SHE'D **LEARNED** THE DIFFERENCE BETWEEN SAVING SOMEONE AND KILLING THEM.

BECAUSE OF WHAT WE'D DONE, BIZARROGIRL HAD **GROWN** INTO SOMETHING **NEW**.

SHE TOLD ME SHE WANTED TO LIVE THE REST OF HER LIFE IN THIS CAVE, PUNISHING HERSELF FOR KILLING THAT MAN. SAID IT WAS ONLY RIGHT.

I DIDN'T TELL HER THAT'S **EXACTLY** HOW I FELT AFTER NEW KRYPTON. AFTER MY PEOPLE KILLED **THOUSANDS** OF INNOCENT BYSTANDERS.

AFTER MY MOTHER DIED BECAUSE OF WHAT I'D DONE.

FINALLY, SHE LOOKED ME STRAIGHT IN THE EYE AND ASKED:

DOES SELF-PUNISHMENT **END**, SUPERGIRL?

EARTH. METROPOLIS.

"NORRIE! I'M GOING TO NEED THAT PAPERWORK BEFORE YOU LEAVE!"

SURE THING, MS. LANG!

AND DON'T FORGET YOUR *UMBRELLA!* IT'S *REALLY* COMING DOWN NOW--

--OKAY, WHO TRACKED WATER INTO MY *OFFICE?* VERY UNCOOL, GUYS!

THAT WAS PROBABLY *MY* FAULT.

CAT? WHY ARE YOU SITTING IN MY OFFICE? IN THE *DARK?*

I NEED TO TALK TO YOU, LANA, ABOUT SOMETHING I *OVERHEARD.*

WELL, CAN IT WAIT UNTIL TOMORROW? I'M TRYING TO GET MY STAFF OUT OF HERE BEFORE THE RAIN GETS ANY *WORSE.*

I WAS OUT WALKING JUST NOW. THINKING.

...OKAY. THINKING ABOUT *WHAT?*

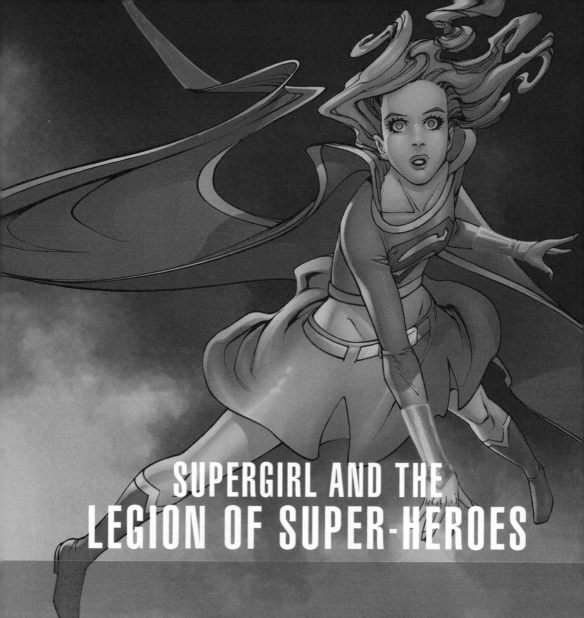

SUPERGIRL AND THE
LEGION OF SUPER-HEROES

MATT CAMP & MARCO RUDY
artists

BLOND with **BRAD ANDERSON**
colorists

STEVE WANDS
letterer

AMY REEDER, RICHARD FRIEND & GUY MAJOR
cover

EARTH.

THE 30TH CENTURY.

METROPOLIS.

--I *KNOW* HE IS. BUT IF I CAN'T KEEP HER ON, WHERE *ELSE* CAN I FIND INEXPENSIVE *HELP?*

MOM?

THEY CAN'T KEEP MAKING LAWS LIKE THAT... NO, I DON'T *EXPECT* THEM TO, IT'S JUST THAT--

...MOM?

WHAT *IS* IT, CARTAR?!

LOOK!!! UP IN THE SKY!

WHAT IS IT?

IT'S A BIRD!

BIRDS DON'T LOOK LIKE THAT. *MUST* BE A SKYBUS.

NO, IT'S NOT. IT'S... IT'S...

...IT'S COMING THIS *WAY!*

BYSTANDERS ON THE STREET BELOW!

COSMIC BOY
A.KA.: ROKK KRINN
HOMEWORLD: BRAAL
ABILITIES: MAGNETISM MANIPULATION

GUYS, WE'RE GONNA NEED MORE DEBRIS-CONTROL!

OUR FEARLESS LEADER CAN'T HANDLE *EVERYTHING*? SHOCKING.

LIGHTNING LAD
A.KA.: GARTH RANZZ
HOMEWORLD: WINATH
ABILITIES: ELECTRICAL GENERATION AND DIRECTION

IF HE CAN'T STAND THE *HEAT*, MAYBE WE SHOULD VOTE IN SOMEONE WHO *CAN*.

SUN BOY
A.KA: DIRK MORGNA
HOMEWORLD: EARTH
ABILITIES: SOLAR ENERGY GENERATION AND MANIPULATION

CHAMELEON BOY
A.KA: REEP DAGGLE
HOMEWORLD: DURLA
ABILITIES: SHAPESHIFTING

EVACUATE IN A *CAREFUL* AND ORDERLY FASHION. HELP THOSE WHO HAVE FALLEN.

ROKK'S DOING WHAT HE *CAN*, BOYS.

SATURN GIRL
A.KA: IMRA ARDEEN
HOMEWORLD: TITAN
ABILITIES: TELEPATHY

AHHH!

PHANTOM GIRL
A.KA: TINYA WAZZO
HOMEWORLD: BGZTL
ABILITIES: INTANGIBILITY

CAN YOU... KEEP THE *STRUCTURE*... INTACT, COS?

WORKING ON IT! COLOSSAL BOY, WE COULD *USE* A HAND RIGHT ABOUT NOW--

SORRY. HAD TO FLY AHEAD...

...IT TAKES *TIME* TO GET UP TO THIS SIZE.

CHROOOM

COLOSSAL BOY
A.K.A: GIM ALLON
HOMEWORLD: EARTH
ABILITIES: GIANT GROWTH

CAN YOU HOLD ON TO ALL OF THAT? IT'S PRETTY HEAVY.

I *GOT* IT, S.G.

NICE WORK, LEGIONNAIRES. SUPERGIRL, THANK YOU AGAIN FOR *HELPING.*

JUST TRYING TO PULL MY OWN *WEIGHT* WHILE I'M HERE.

FALLING SATELLITE? *EASY* FOR US. ANY IDEA WHAT BROUGHT THIS HUNKA JUNK DOWN--

WAIT. DO YOU HEAR THAT?

HEAR WHA--

SHHRRRPP

SOMETHING'S HAPPENING *INSIDE!*

133

IT'S FUNNY...

...THIS IS SORT OF HOW I GOT HERE IN THE FIRST PLACE.

I WAS FLYING BACK FROM BIZARRO WORLD* WHEN *SOMETHING* IN MY SHIP MALFUNCTIONED...

VEET VEET VEET VEET

UHH, THAT'S NOT GOOD.

*SEE LAST WEEK'S *SUPERGIRL* #57 --MATT

CHROOON

...AND IT EXPLODED.

SO WHEN I WOKE *UP*...

UNNH... SHOULD'VE KNOWN BETTER THAN TO TRUST *BIZARRO* TO HELP ME REBUILD THAT STUPID ROCKET...

...I WOKE UP IN THE 30TH CENTURY.

WHAT? *WHAT?*

...*WHAT?!*

IT WASN'T THE 30TH CENTURY I'D VISITED BEFORE, EITHER...

I *HEAR* YOUR CONFUSION, SUPERGIRL, BUT DO NOT BE *AFRAID.*

IF SHE STAYS-- AND SHE *SHOULDN'T*-- IT'LL BE JUST AS DANGEROUS AS WHEN WE ALLOW SUPERBOY TO VISIT--

OH, C'MON, BRAIN! YOU *ALWAYS* HAVE FUN WHEN SUPERBOY'S HERE!

DO YOU UNDERSTAND HOW *HARD* IT IS TO MAINTAIN THE *TIMELINE* EVERY TIME WE LET SUPERBOY HANG AROUND?! THE NOVIKOV AND BLINOVITCH EFFECTS *ALONE* TAKE ME *HOURS* TO ACCOUNT FOR!

AND WHAT IF SHE GETS LOOSE IN THE *SUPERMAN MUSEUM* AND LEARNS ABOUT HER OWN *FUTURE*, GARTH?!

IF SHE LEARNS IN *ADVANCE* ABOUT "THE SCION OF SUPERMAN" OR "THE DEADLY DAY OF THE DOLLMAKER" OR "LEX LUTHOR'S *OTHER* SON," THOSE THINGS MIGHT NOT HAPPEN. AND THEY *HAVE* TO HAPPEN!

THEY'RE *SET EVENTS* IN THE TIMESTREAM, AND IF WE *DISRUPT* THAT--

EASY. WE GET IMRA TO DO THE MEMORY TRICK THAT SHE DOES ON KAL, AND ALL OF THIS WILL JUST SEEM LIKE A *DREAM* TO HER.

AND I THOUGHT *YOU* WERE SUPPOSED TO BE THE *GENIUS* ON THIS TEAM.

NO, LIGHTNING LAD, THAT'S NOT *GOOD* ENOUGH. WE NEED TO SEND HER BACK *RIGHT NOW*, BEFORE THIS GETS ANY *WORSE!*

AND WHO *KNOWS* IF SHE EVEN *WANTS* TO STAY HERE--

ACTUALLY...

...I'D LIKE TO.

BUT *ONLY* IF IT'S OKAY WITH YOU, BRAINIAC 5.

UM... I...I... UH...

FINE.

BUT SUPERBOY *CANNOT* COME TO THE FUTURE WHILE *YOU'RE* HERE.

ONE POTENTIAL THREAT TO THE SPACE/TIME CONTINUUM AT A TIME.

I *KNEW* HIM, THOUGH. BRAINIAC 5. I'D MET HIM BEFORE...

--LEGION WILL TAKE *FULL* RESPONSIBILITY, AS WELL AS HELP TO *REPAIR* THE DAMAGED BUILDINGS.

SO I KNEW HOW *ANGEROUS* E COULD BE.

YOUR REFLEXES APPEAR TO BE NORMAL, SO WE CAN RULE OUT A *CONCUSSION*--

YES, FINE, GREAT! I HAVE *WORK* TO DO, THEN, SO IF YOU'LL *PLEASE* LET ME GET BACK TO IT, WE'LL ALL SLEEP WELL TONIGHT.

HE CHECKS OUT?

GOOD. WE NEED TO TALK TO HIM.

WE COULD START WITH WHAT YOU WERE *DOING* UP THERE.

TALK ABOUT *WHAT*, COSMIC BOY?

IT'S CALLED *RESEARCH.* I WAS TRYING TO SOLVE A *SCIENTIFIC IMPOSSIBILITY* THROUGH OBSERVATION AND *EXPERIMENTATION*--

YOUR "RESEARCH" COULDA LEVELED THE CITY, MORON!

YOUR RECKLESSNESS NEARLY GOT COLOSSAL BOY KILLED--

"RECKLESSNESS"?

IT. WAS. AN. ACCIDENT!

I TOOK EVERY SAFETY PRECAUTION POSSIBLE! IT'S NOT MY FAULT THE ARTIFACT BEHAVED UNCONTROL-LABLY. KIND OF LIKE SOME LEGIONNAIRES I KNOW...

UNCONTROL THIS, YOU KNOW-IT-ALL SON-OF-A--

SKAZZZ

AAHH!

BRAINIAC 5 SAID IT WAS AN ACCIDENT, LIGHTNING LAD. ONE WHERE NO ONE GOT HURT, I MIGHT ADD. SO IT'S TIME TO EASE DOWN.

CLEAR?

C-CRYSTAL.

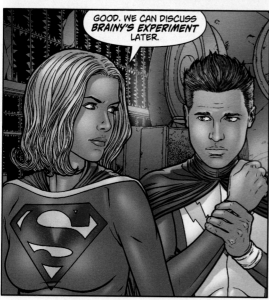

GOOD. WE CAN DISCUSS BRAINY'S EXPERIMENT LATER.

RIGHT NOW, LET'S ALL CHIP IN AND PUT THIS PLACE BACK TOGETHER. WE WORK AS A TEAM, AND IT'LL TAKE NO TIME--

LEGIONNAIRES!

YOU ARE TO *EVACUATE* THIS AREA *IMMEDIATELY.*

YOU MUST BE *JOKING,* OFFICERS. WE'RE HERE TO *HELP* YOU. WE'RE GOING TO PUT THIS BLOCK BACK TOGETHER.

I'M WARNING YOU, SUPERGIRL. EVACUATE, OR I *WILL* FIRE ON YOU.

SUPERGIRL, DON'T.

WHAT? WE'RE TRYING TO *HELP*--

HEY!

I'VE SEEN THE TAPES. I KNOW THAT DIDN'T HURT YOU, SUPERGIRL, BUT I WANTED TO MAKE MYSELF *UNDERSTOOD.*

LEAVE. RIGHT. NOW.

THE LEGIONNAIRES HAVE DIPLOMATIC IMMUNITY. YOU DON'T, KRYPTONIAN. WE DON'T *WANT* YOUR HELP, NOR DO WE NEED IT.

UNDERSTOOD.

C'MON, LEGIONNAIRES. LET'S GO.

I'D LOVE TO JOIN YOU, BUT I HAVE TO FIND THE PIECES OF THAT STATUE. IF I DON'T RETURN IT TO THE BROCIAN EMBASSY, I'LL--

--HEY!

YOU CAN COME BACK AND LOOK LATER, BRAINY. I'M SURE THE PIECES WILL STILL BE THERE.

XENOPHOBIA, HUH?

EVERYWHERE AND EVERYWHEN YOU GO, THERE'S ALWAYS SOMEBODY TRYING TO RUN YOU OFF.

HEY, WHAT DOES HE MEAN HE'S "SEEN THE TAPES"?

THAT WAS A CLOSE ONE, HUH? DID YOU SEE HOW ANGRY SUPERGIRL LOOKED AT THE COMMANDER?

≥KAFF KAFF KAFF≤

SOMETHING STUCK IN YOUR THROAT, CARTAR?

≥KAFF KAFF KAFF≤

YOU OKAY, BUCK?

YEAH. I'M FINE NOW.

YEAH. I'M FINE NOW.

COMPLETELY FINE.

COMPLETELY FINE.

I'M NOT REALLY SURE WHY I STAYED.

I GUESS IT JUST SEEMED LIKE A NICE CHANGE.

THE THINGS THE LEGION DID, THE ADVENTURES THEY HAD...EVEN THE VILLAINS THEY FOUGHT...IT ALL JUST SEEMED SO...

...INNOCENT COMPARED TO SOME OF THE STUFF I'VE HAD TO DEAL WITH.

NEW KRYPTON... REACTRON...

LET'S *GO*, LEGION!

NO *INTERGALACTIC* WARS HERE. MURDERS WERE FEWER AND FARTHER BETWEEN IN THE FUTURE.

IT FELT...*RIGHT* FOR ME TO BE HERE.

AFTER A *MONTH*, THEY MADE ME AN *OFFICIAL* MEMBER OF THE TEAM.

BUT THEY DIDN'T JUST *HAND* ME THE RING... I HAD TO *EARN* IT.

WHETHER IT WAS BY FINDING *ANCIENT* ARTIFACTS...

SUPER SPECIAL DELIVERY: ONE *SWORD* OF KING ARTHUR!

YES!

...HELPING BREAK UP A KRYPTONITE ASTEROID FIELD THREE SECTORS OVER...

MY FORCEFIELD BELT WILL *PROTECT* YOU FROM THE KRYPTONITE RADIATION, SUPERGIRL, BUT YOU'VE *STILL* GOT TO BE CAREFUL!

OKAY, BRAINY, I GOT IT!

...TAKING ON THE *VILLAINS* OF THE 30TH CENTURY...

YOU-- SHALL--NOT-- PASS!

...OR EVEN SPENDING *QUALITY* TIME WITH THE GIRLS ON THE TEAM.

THAT'S ACTUALLY A REALLY GOOD LOOK FOR YOU, EMM.

YOU THINK SO?

SURE. YOU CAN'T REALLY *LIE* TO A TELEPATH, CAN YOU?

IT'S FUNNY, THOUGH.

THE STARS ARE SLIGHTLY *DIFFERENT* IN THE FUTURE, TOO. THE PEOPLE OF METROPOLIS SPEAK AN *UNFAMILIAR* LANGUAGE.

EVEN BEING WITH A TEAM OF PEOPLE THAT'RE LIKE ME... EVEN AFTER THEY'VE TRIED SO HARD TO MAKE ME FEEL WELCOME...I STILL FEEL...

...I DUNNO...

...KINDA LONESOME.

HM.

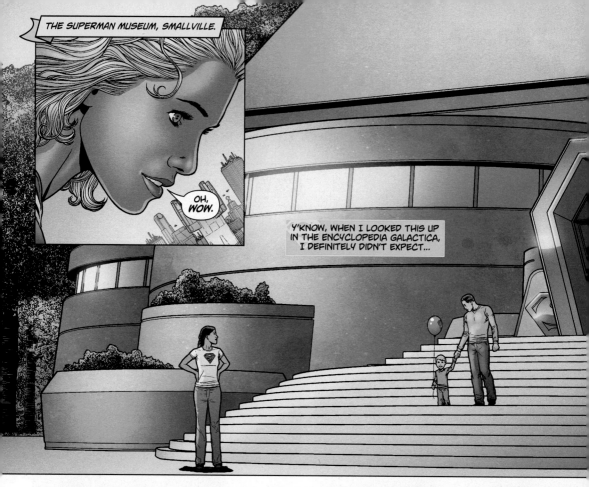

THE SUPERMAN MUSEUM, SMALLVILLE.

OH, WOW.

Y'KNOW, WHEN I LOOKED THIS UP IN THE ENCYCLOPEDIA GALACTICA, I DEFINITELY DIDN'T EXPECT...

NO WONDER THEY DIDN'T WANT TO TELL ME ABOUT THIS PLACE.

...WELL, ANYTHING LIKE THIS.

HOW DO YOU TELL SOMEONE THEIR COUSIN IS ONE OF THE BIGGEST HEROES IN HISTORY? HE'S ALMOST *DEIFIED* HERE!

⸘KZZT⸘ HELLO THERE, STRANGE VISITOR!

WELCOME TO THE *SUPERMAN MUSEUM!* I'M JIMMY OLSEN.

A THOUSAND YEARS AGO, I WAS SUPERMAN'S *CONFIDANT* AND *BEST FRIEND.*

REALLY? I NEVER GOT THAT FROM THE TWO OF YOU.

HA HA! YOU'RE A JOKESTER. I'LL BE YOUR *HOLOGRAPHIC GUIDE* THIS MORNING. YOU GOT ANY QUESTIONS, ALL YOU GOTTA DO IS *ASK.* WHAT WOULD YOU LIKE TO SEE *FIRST?*

HM. JIMMY, WHAT CAN YOU TELL ME ABOUT SUPER-GIRL?

OH, THE TALE OF SUPERMAN'S COUSIN IS AN *EPIC* AND *SAD* ONE. ARE YOU SURE YOU WANT TO HEAR IT? WOULDN'T YOU RATHER SEE THE HALL OF 1,000 OLSENS?

EACH ANIMA-TRONIC ROBOT IS BASED ON ONE OF MY *CRAZY* ADVENTURES--

JIMMY. SUPERGIRL. PLEASE.

I CAN SEE YOU'RE SET ON THIS. OKAY, THEN.

FOLLOW ME.

--PARENTS SENT HER AWAY FROM ARGO CITY IN A ROCKET SO SHE WOULDN'T BE CAPTURED BY BRAINIAC LIKE THE REST OF THE KANDORIANS.

SHE CAME TO EARTH AND ALSO BECAME A HERO, STRIVING TO LIVE UP TO THE SYMBOL OF THE HOUSE OF EL--ONE THAT SUPERMAN HAD MADE INTO A SYMBOL OF HOPE.

TRAGICALLY, DURING ONE OF THE GREATEST BATTLES IN HISTORY, SHE WAS KILLED STOPPING THE WORST THREAT THE EARTH HAD EVER KNOWN, GIVING HER LIFE TO SAVE HER ADOPTED PLANET.

THAT'S WHY THE SUPERMAN MUSEUM COMMEMORATES HER COURAGE AND HEROISM IN LIFE WITH THE *"SUPERGIRL MEMORIAL HALL."*

...WHAT?

THIS...*THIS* IS WHY THEY WERE KEEPING ME AWAY FROM HERE.

I GET IT, THEY DIDN'T WANT ME TO KNOW TOO MUCH ABOUT MY FUTURE, BUT THIS...

THIS IS IMPORTANT.

I *REFUSE* TO LET THEM KEEP THIS FROM ME. THIS COULD CHANGE EVERYTHING.

THIS...

...THIS...

OH, ☿‼⎍.

...THIS IS HOW I DIE.

MISS, ARE YOU ALL RIGHT? YOU REALLY SPED OFF!

YEAH, I...UH...

...I SORT OF THREW UP BACK THERE.

OH, DON'T WORRY ABOUT IT! WE HAVE A *MARVEL-OUS* CLEANING CREW! THEY'RE GREAT AT PICKING UP AFTER OUR VISITORS!

I'VE GOT TO GET OUT OF HERE. I'VE GOT TO GO *BACK* AS SOON AS POSSIBLE...

BACK, MISS? WHERE WOULD YOU LIKE TO GO BACK *TO*? I CAN SWITCH ON SUPERMAN'S HALL OF VILLAINS FOR YOU!

THE ANIMATRONIC SHOW *THEY* CAN PUT ON IS BOTH *ASTOUNDING* AND SCARY--

SHUT UP, JIMMY!

VZZZZAT

--FFZZZT OKAY! I CAN SEE YOU'D RATHER LOOK AROUND FOR YOURSELF.

HAVE A GOOD DAY, AND THANKS FOR COMING TO THE *SUPERMAN MUSEUM!*

I...I JUST CAN'T BELIEVE IT...WHAT ELSE CAN GO WRONG TODAY?

ZZZTT-- *SUPERGIRL!* LEGION S.O.S!

BRAINY? WHAT'S GOING ON?

WE NEED YOU BACK IN METROPOLIS! LIKE, *RIGHT NOW!*

I'M SORT OF...*BUSY* AT THE MOMENT, BRAINY. ARE YOU *SURE* YOU NEED ME?

I'M PRETTY *DAMN* SURE!

WE'VE GOT A **FULL-SCALE** RIOT GOING ON, AND WE **REALLY** NEED SOMEONE WITH YOUR **STRENGTH** LEVELS!

FWOOH

WHAT'S WRONG WITH THEM?

I DON'T KNOW YET. I'M GETTING TRACES OF A STRANGE SUBSTANCE IN THE AIR, THOUGH.

SOME SORT OF MIND CONTROL GAS?

MY FORCE-FIELD BELT SEEMS TO BE PROTECTING ME FROM IT.

WHERE ARE THE OTHER LEGIONNAIRES?

MOST OF THEM HAVE ALREADY **SUCCUMBED** TO IT--

FZZAT

OW! WHAT DID YOU DO?

WHAT? I DIDN'T DO **ANYTHING**!

YOU **SHOCKED** ME--

SHE COMES!

SSHZZZAT

SHE COMES! S'TANICULE GYRSTRESS COMES!

SHE COMES!

SHE COMES!

FWASSSSHH

THAT DOESN'T LOOK GOOD!

I DON'T KNOW *WHO* YOU ARE, BUT I'M GOING TO KICK YOUR HORNS BACK INTO THAT RIFT--

NO, YOU'RE *NOT!*

BRAINY--?

I KNOW WHO THAT *IS*, KARA, AND WE'RE *NOT* ABOUT TO STICK AROUND.

T.TK VEET

WHAT ARE YOU--

153

YES. I'VE BEEN DEVELOPING A *CRUDE* FORM OF PERSONALIZED *TIME TRAVEL*. OBVIOUSLY, IT STILL NEEDS *WORK*.

HOW FAR DID WE *GO?* WHAT HAPPENED HERE? WHERE DID EVERYONE *GO?*

WE'RE *FOUR DAYS* INTO THE FUTURE. WHAT WE SAW WAS THE ARRIVAL OF S'TANICULE GYRSTRESS. *"SATAN GIRL,"* AS SHE'S KNOWN IN SOME CIRCLES, IS THE BROCIAN GODDESS OF LOVE AND DEATH.

DEATH? SO WHAT MAKES YOU SO SURE SHE HASN'T *KILLED* OUR FRIENDS? AND MORE IMPORTANTLY, HOW DID SHE GET TO *EARTH?*

WELL, THAT PART MIGHT ACTUALLY BE *MY* FAULT. THE STATUE I WAS EXPERIMENTING ON IN MY LAB A FEW WEEKS AGO WAS A TRIBUTE TO THE GODDESS.

SO?

SO WHEN I BOMBARDED IT WITH CHRONONS, I MIGHT'VE... WELL, *CALLED* HER HERE.

OKAY, LET'S REVIEW.

YOU, BRAINIAC 5, WHILE EXPERIMENTING ON A SUPPOSEDLY "MAGICAL" STATUE, BOMBARDED IT WITH TIMESTREAM ENERGY, THEREBY SUMMONING AN ALIEN DEATH GODDESS.

MM.

THEN, WHEN SHE SHOWS UP AND STARTS POSSESSING OUR FRIENDS, YOUR FIRST INCLINATION IS NOT TO STAY AND *FIGHT,* BUT RUN AWAY INTO THE TIMESTREAM.

WHICH PRETTY MUCH ENSURES THAT SHE ENSLAVES THE ENTIRE EARTH.

OH, I DOUBT THE *ENTIRE* EARTH'S BEEN ENSLAVED BY THIS POINT, SUPERGIRL. I MEAN, SHE'S ONLY HAD A FEW DAYS.

EVEN IF HER FORCES GREW *EXPONENTIALLY* EVERY DAY, THERE WOULD STILL BE *POCKETS* OF FREE PEOPLE OUT THERE SOMEWHERE--

NNN...

I'M WHAT?

BRAINY, WAKE *UP!* YOU'RE ALIVE!

I'M...I'M *FINE!* IT WORKED!

IT WORKED!

YEAH, WE DID IT!

I MEAN, OF *COURSE* IT WORKED. IT *WAS* MY PLAN, AFTER ALL.

OF COURSE.

SO, GUYS...

...WHAT ARE WE ALL SO *EXCITED* ABOUT?

HAMMERSMITH TOWER.

HOME OF LANA AND LINDA LANG.

THE PRESENT.

BOOM

--ASIDE FROM ALL OF *THAT*, I HAD A REALLY GREAT TIME!

WELL, WE AIM TO *PLEASE*, SUPERGIRL. SORRY THINGS GOT PRETTY *HAIRY* THERE FOR YOU.

THAT'S OKAY. WISH I COULD REMEMBER EVERYTHING THAT HAPPENED, THOUGH.

WELL, TIME TRAVEL CAN TAKE A *TOLL* ON YOUR MIND...

...ESPECIALLY SKIPPING AROUND *UNPROTECTED* LIKE YOU DID.

HMPH. MY MEMORY SEEMS FINE.

ANYWAY, THANKS FOR THE RIDE *HOME*. I'M REALLY HAPPY I GOT TO HANG OUT WITH YOU GUYS!

ANYTIME!

HEY, BRAINY?

YES?

I KNOW OUR JAUNT INTO DYSTOPIAN HELL WASN'T EXACTLY THE BEST "DATE," BUT IF YOU WANNA COME BACK AND TAKE ME ON A REAL ONE SOMETIME, I'D BE ALL FOR IT.

I--I--

WHAT LOVERBOY IS TRYING TO SAY HERE, SUPERGIRL, IS THAT HE'D LOVE TO.

WE GOTTA GO NOW, THOUGH, OR ELSE THE TIME-SPACE EMPORIUM OR WHATEVER MIGHT COLLAPSE AROUND US.

SHE-- SHE *KISSED* ME!

I KNOW, BRAINY. YOU'LL GET USED TO IT.

BOOM

BYE, GUYS!

"FOR THE RECORD, I DON'T LIKE WHAT WE *DID* BACK THERE."

IT *HAD* TO BE DONE, ROKK.

I COULD SEE IT IN HER MIND. SOMETIME DURING HER TIME IN OUR ERA, SUPERGIRL FOUND OUT ABOUT HER DEATH.

I HAD TO WIPE THOSE MEMORIES AWAY. SOMEDAY SHE'LL LIVE THROUGH THOSE EVENTS, AND THAT MIGHT SPARK THE MEMORY IN HER HEAD.

UNTIL THEN, THOUGH...

"...SHE'LL HAVE A MUCH HAPPIER LIFE NOT KNOWING HER OWN FUTURE."

BRAINIAC 5 PERSONAL LOG #10272010: SATURN GIRL SAYS WE SHOULD NEVER TELL SUPERGIRL ABOUT HER FUTURE FOR HER OWN GOOD.

BUT SOMEONE HAS TO WARN HER--EITHER DIRECTLY OR INDIRECTLY--ABOUT THE TERRIBLE THINGS THAT WILL UNFOLD SOON.

THAT SOMEONE WILL BE *ME.* I PROMISE YOU, KARA.

YOU WON'T HAVE TO DIE ALONE. NOT LIKE YOU DID IN THE *HISTORY BOOKS...*

DAY OF THE DOLLMAKER

PART ONE: TOYING WITH EMOTIONS

JAMAL IGLE
penciller

JON SIBAL
inker

BLOND
colorist

TRAVIS LANHAM
letterer

AMY REEDER & GUY MAJOR
cover

TODAY.

CHRISTMAS EVE EVE.

GRANT, CAT REPORTER DAILY PLANET

HELLO.

T-TALK? ABOUT WHAT?

YOU KNOW ME, DON'T YOU, TOYMAN? YOU REMEMBER WHAT HAPPENED BETWEEN US ALL THOSE YEARS AGO.

EVEN IF YOU ONLY SAW IT THROUGH YOUR ROBOT'S SYNTHETIC EYES.

WE'RE HERE BECAUSE IT LOOKS LIKE YOU'VE BEEN BUSY AGAIN. PLAYING PIED PIPER TO THE CHILDREN OF METROPOLIS--

WHA-WHAT? NO, I'VE BEEN A GOOD BOY SINCE I GOT PUT BACK IN ARKHAM! I'VE DONE NOTHING WRONG!

GUARD! GUARD! THESE PEOPLE HAVE COME TO HARASS ME--

"NOTHING WRONG"?! ARE YOU KIDDING ME?!

UNNH--!

AND HOW DO WE KNOW YOU'RE EVEN THE REAL WINSLOW SCHOTT?!

I'VE SEEN ONE OF YOUR ROBOTS BEFORE-- NO, TWO OF THEM. ONE HERE IN GOTHAM, THE OTHER ON NEW KRYPTON.

AND THAT ONE HAD A PART IN MY WORLD'S DESTRUCTION. A SMALL PART, SURE, BUT AN IMPORTANT ONE.

...AND I'LL START PROBING TO MAKE SURE YOU'RE REAL.

SSSS

NOW THEN. CONSIDER THIS AN INFORMAL INTERVIEW, WINSLOW.

I JUST HAVE A FEW QUESTIONS...

YOUR WORK IS VERY WELL MADE. IMPOSSIBLE TO TELL APART FROM REAL, LIVE HUMAN BEINGS, EVEN WITH MY X-RAY VISION.

SO PLEASE. ANSWER MS. GRANT'S QUESTIONS, OR ELSE ANOTHER OUTBURST LIKE THAT WILL LEAD ME TO BELIEVE YOU'RE ONE OF SCHOTT'S AUTOMATONS...

I-I'M REAL. I SWEAR!

...ABOUT THESE *CHILDREN*. DO YOU RECOGNIZE THEM?

N-NO. WHO ARE THEY?

YOU *KNOW* WHO THEY ARE.

ELI BROWN. JULIAN THOMAS. TRINA CODY. ALL OF THEM TAKEN OFF THE STREETS OF METROPOLIS.

BY *YOU.*

NO, I WOULDN'T HURT CHILDREN. I *LOVE* THEM, THEY'RE MY *FRIENDS!*

ADULTS ARE THE ONES I *HATE.* ADULTS LIKE YOU, MS. GRANT.

YOU, I DON'T LIKE.

IS THAT WHY YOU SENT ME THE DOLLS?

DOLLS?

YES...

THIS WAS THE FIRST ONE YOU SENT.*

I DIDN'T THINK MUCH ABOUT IT. I THOUGHT IT WAS A MISGUIDED MESSAGE FROM A FAN. I THREW IT AWAY.

BUT SOMETHING ABOUT IT *BOTHERED* ME. I FISHED IT OUT OF THE TRASHCAN AND TOOK IT HOME.

THAT WAS THE SAME DAY TRINA CODY WENT MISSING.

*WAAAAY BACK IN *SUPERGIRL #38!* --MATTHUSELAH

...*THIS* ONE ARRIVED.

YOU KNOW *DAMN* WELL HOW I DID. YOU SENT IT TO MY OFFICE. I TOOK IT HOME AND OPENED IT AND IT ATTACKED.

I ATTACKED BACK.

MM. THIS IS *VERY* SIMILAR TO SOME OF MY *EARLY* DESIGNS--

THIS ONE ARRIVED THE SAME DAY THAT JULIAN THOMAS WENT MISSING. HIS MOTHER TURNED AROUND WHILE THEY WERE SHOPPING AND HE WAS GONE.

THEN FINALLY...

THE SAME DAY ELI BROWN WENT MISSING.

...IMPOSSIBLE.

MAY I SEE THAT, PLEASE?

HOW DID YOU COME INTO POSSESSION OF THIS?

VOCAL PATTERN CONFIRMED. ACTIVATING MESSAGE.

HELLO, WINSLOW!

TOOK YOUR EYES OFF THE *PRIZE* KEWPIE DOLL, DIDN'T YOU?!

AAAHH!

YO! CHUCKY!

EEP!

VZZASSSH

WHO *ARE* YOU?

OHHHH, THAT'S THE *MILLION-DOLLAR* QUESTION, ISN'T IT?

AND HERE MS. GRANT THOUGHT *YOU* WOULD BE THE ONE TO GET HER OUT OF THIS TREE, AND YOU'VE JUST MELTED SOME KEY EVIDENCE. HOW SAD.

BYE BYE, GIRLS! BE SEEING YOUUU...

"HUGE NEWS OUT OF S.T.A.R. LABS METROPOLIS TODAY--"

THIS WILL FURTHER HER STUDIES IN REHABILITATING METAHUMANS DRIVEN MENTALLY INSANE FROM THEIR POWERS, AND-- *KZZAT*

--AS DR. KIMIYO HOSHI ANNOUNCED PROGRESS IN METAHUMAN GENETICS THAT WILL ENABLE HER TO POSSIBLY *REMOVE* THE METAHUMAN GENOME.

WELL.

THAT COULD'VE GONE *BETTER.*

YOU *THINK?* GUESS WE CAN TAKE TOYMAN OFF THE LIST OF PEOPLE WHO MIGHT'VE MADE THOSE DOLLS.

AND AS SOON AS HE'S OUT OF THE WOODS, I'M GOING BACK TO METROPOLIS TO LOOK FOR THOSE *KIDS.*

...UNLESS SCHOTT'S STILL PLAYING US FROM ALL ANGLES.

A KNIFE THROUGH THE CHEST DOESN'T SEEM LIKE "PLAYING AN ANGLE," CAT. WE'RE LUCKY HE'S *ALIVE*.

ARE YOU SURE HE WAS THE *REAL* TOYMAN?

VERY.

...SO HE GOT HURT BECAUSE OF US.

I GUESS THE QUESTION NOW BECOMES, WHO DID YOU WRITE AN ARTICLE ABOUT THIS TIME, AND WHO DID IT PISS OFF?

DON'T TAKE THAT *TONE* WITH *ME*, YOUNG LADY. I'M A *RESPECTED* REPORTER. *WHY* DO YOU ASSUME IT WAS MY WRITING--

"*RESPECTED*"?! SAYS THE WOMAN WHO WRITES ABOUT HOW *SHORT* MY SKIRT IS EVERY OTHER DAY, THEN BLACKMAILS MY FRIENDS TO GET ME TO PULL HER FAT OUT OF THE FIRE?!

WELL, IF YOU'D BE MORE *CAREFUL* ABOUT HOW YOU *FLY*, MAYBE I WOULDN'T *HAVE* TO WRITE SUCH THINGS.

OH, SO IT'S *MY FAULT* YOU WRITE SUCH HATEFUL TRASH ABOUT ME?! MY FAULT THAT I'M YOUR *PERSONAL* TARGET TO SNIPE AT--

NOT THAT I NEED TO VALIDATE MY POINTS TO A TEENAGE GIRL WHO DOESN'T EVEN KNOW BELLY SHIRTS ARE *OUT* THIS DECADE, BUT...

WHAT I WRITE IS NOT *HATEFUL*, IT'S *FACTUAL*. LIVES ARE AT RISK *EVERY TIME* YOUR INEXPERIENCED *BLUNDERING* COMES ON-SCENE.

IT'S MY *DUTY* TO REPORT IT. IF IT SEEMS LIKE YOU'RE A *TARGET*, MAYBE YOU SHOULD GET BETTER AT YOUR *JOB*.

AND I'M NOT *BLACKMAILING* ANYONE. I MERELY ASKED LANA TO ASK HER FRIEND TO HELP ME.

I WISH TO GOD IN HEAVEN I KNEW HOW TO GET A HOLD OF *SUPERMAN*, BUT I COULDN'T FIND JIMMY OR THAT SIGNAL WATCH OF HIS, AND LOIS TOLD ME SHE WASN'T SUPERMAN'S *SECRETARY*.

SO YOU HAD TO SETTLE FOR ME. MUST BE *SO HARD* FOR YOU, WORKING WITH "A TARTED-UP TEENAGER WITH SOMETHING TO PROVE."

HM?

THAT'S WHAT YOU SAID ABOUT ME IN YOUR FIRST ARTICLE. "WHY THE WORLD DOESN'T NEED SUPERGIRL."

I CAN HEAR THE DOCTORS FROM HERE. TOYMAN'S STABILIZED.

I AGREED TO PLAY "BAD COP" BECAUSE A DOLL-MAKING KILLER IS TAKING KIDS OFF THE STREETS, AND *YOU'RE* THE ONLY ONE HE'S SENDING CLUES TO.

CRIMINALS HAVE FRIENDS, THOUGH. SOMEONE IN METROPOLIS KNOWS *SOMETHING* ABOUT THESE DOLLS. I'LL FIND THEM, AND THEY'LL LEAD ME TO THIS GUY.

IN THE MEANTIME, I'LL CALL THE JUSTICE LEAGUE AND DO MY BEST TO KEEP *ARKHAM* FROM PRESSING CHARGES AGAINST US.

HM. AFTER YOUR PERFORMANCE TODAY, I'M STILL NOT SURE *ANYONE* DOES.

THAT'S IT. I'M *GONE.*

WHAT? BUT YOU CAN'T--

BUT-- BUT *WAIT!* I NEED--

YOU NEED TO LEAVE ME ALONE, IS WHAT YOU *NEED* TO DO.

THAT DETECTIVE WANTS TO SPEAK TO US, BUT SINCE THIS IS *YOUR* MESS AND I WANT TO GET BACK TO *METROPOLIS,* I'LL LEAVE YOU TO DEAL WITH IT.

FAR AS I'M CONCERNED, THIS PARTNERSHIP IS *OVER.*

WAIT! WHAT IF--

--WHAT IF I NEED TO GET A HOLD OF YOU AGAIN?

MS. GRANT?

HARVEY BULLOCK, GOTHAM P.D. I GOT A FEW QUESTIONS FOR YA.

"I JUST *CAN'T BELIEVE* HER."

A KID? SOMEONE AGREED TO *MATE* WITH THAT WOMAN?

KARA...

I KNOW, I KNOW. UNCALLED FOR. SHE JUST KNOWS HOW TO PUSH MY BUTTONS.

EEP!

AND SOMEONE'S PUSHING *HER* BUTTONS WITH TOYMAN.

HER SON ADAM WAS KILLED RESCUING A GROUP OF CHILDREN WHO WERE KIDNAPPED BY ONE OF TOYMAN'S MALFUNCTIONING ROBOTS.

THE ROBOT CUT HIS THROAT.*

*SEE *SUPERMAN* #84.

CAT *CHANGED* AFTER THAT.

"SHE DIDN'T *GRIEVE.* INSTEAD, SHE TURNED *HARD.*

"SHE MOVED TO L.A. AND STARTED WRITING FOR *TABLOIDS,* TEARING DOWN ANYONE SHE COULD.

"THE MORE TEEN STARS AND STARLETS SHE SAW PARADING AROUND TOWN, THE ANGRIER AND ANGRIER HER WRITING BECAME."

ANGRIER?

CLARK AND LOIS AND I TALKED A LOT ABOUT THIS.

"CLARK THINKS CAT BECAME ANGRY THAT THOSE TEENS WERE STILL ALIVE TO MAKE MESSES OF THEIR LIVES...

"...AND HER SON WASN'T."

MERRY CHRISTMAS, BABY.

ADAM GRANT
BELOVED SON AND HERO

"ANYWAY, HOW'S YOUR SEARCH COMING ALONG?"

SLOWLY. I'VE GONE THROUGH THE USUAL SUSPECTS, BUT NO ONE SEEMS TO KNOW *WHO* THIS GUY IS OR WHERE THOSE KIDS ARE.

I HOPE YOU *FIND* THOSE CHILDREN. I CAN'T IMAGINE HOW THEIR PARENTS ARE FEELING. CHRISTMAS EVE WITHOUT YOUR CHILD...

SPEAKING OF, ARE YOU EXCITED TO SEE YOUR SON CLARK?

...LANA?

LANA?

I'M HERE. I THINK IT'S GOING TO BE *AWKWARD*, AS MOST THINGS ARE WITH PETE NOW. THAT'S HOW IT GOES WITH *EXES*, I GUESS.

BUT, YES, I'M VERY EXCITED TO SEE MY SON.

CAT DIDN'T SAY ANYTHING MORE ABOUT ME, DID SHE?

NO. I THINK SHE JUST THOUGHT YOU WERE MY *INFORMANT*. LIKE JIMMY IS FOR KAL.

I THINK LINDA LANG'S SAFE FOR NOW.

OKAY. THEN I HOPE I SEE YOU AT MA'S TOMORROW.

AND REMEMBER, KARA, HOLIDAYS ARE ABOUT *FAMILY*.

WELCOME TO *Smallville*

THIS IS PROBABLY A *VERY* HARD TIME OF THE YEAR FOR CAT, SO TRY TO GO EASY ON HER.

...I'LL TRY. THANKS, LANA. FOR EVERYTHING.

DEET

OH, DAMMIT.

WHERE ARE MY *KEYS?* I HOPE I DIDN'T LEAVE THEM AT THE--

FWZT

MMMM...

SNP SNPSNP

MMMMMM--!

HOLY GOD!!

SKRA-ZZZ

MMMMMM!

AND *THAT'S* WHAT YOU GET FOR *STALKING* ME, YOU SON OF A--

OH MY GOD-- ELI! ARE YOU OKAY?! WHAT HAPPENED TO YOU?

DO YOU *LIKE* HIM? HE'S ONE OF MY NEWEST MODELS.

W-WHO...?

LANE,
LOIS
REPORTER
DAILY PLAN

DR. KIMIYO HOSHI

METAHUMAN/
EXTRATERRESTRIAL
STUDIES AND
EXPERIMENTATION

HEY,
SIS...

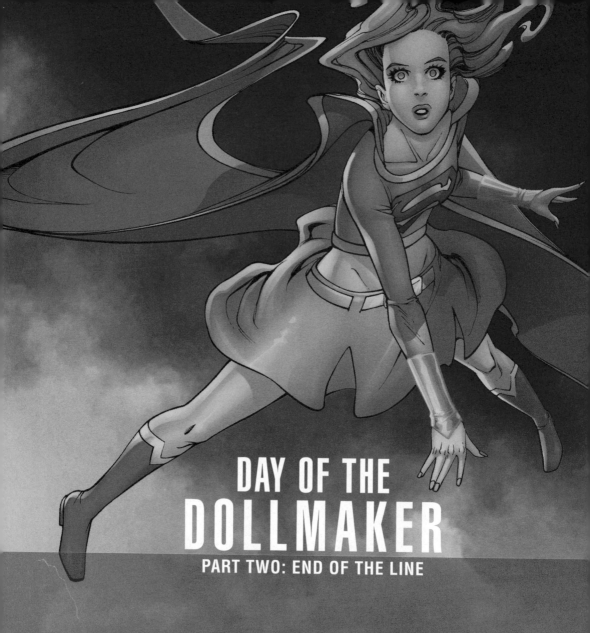

DAY OF THE
DOLLMAKER

PART TWO: END OF THE LINE

JAMAL IGLE
penciller

JON SIBAL & ROBIN RIGGS
inkers

BLOND
colorist

TRAVIS LANHAM
letterer

AMY REEDER, RICHARD FRIEND & GUY MAJOR
cover

THE OUTSKIRTS OF METROPOLIS.

CHRISTMAS EVE.

"I HOPE EVERYONE'S HAVING A **WONDERFUL** HOLIDAY SO **FAR!**"

WE **ARE** ALL HAVING A GOOD TIME, RIGHT?

YOU, ME, AND THE DARING DOLL MEN!

RIIIIIIGHT?!

MM MNNA MLL NMMU.

199

"MM MNNA MLL NMMU," SHE SAYS! I COMPLLLLLETELY AGREE! DON'T YOU?!?

NOW WHAT WAS I SAYING?

OH YES! CHRISTMAS!

DO YOU KNOW WHY CHRISTMAS IS MY FAVORITE HOLIDAY, CAT?

MMF. NMMER.

BECAUSE IT'S MY BIRTHDAY!

AND WE ALL LOVE BIRTHDAYS, DON'T WE?!?

"YES, FATHER MUST'VE BEEN FEELING AMOROUS IN THE SPRINGTIME--LOVE IS IN THE AIR THEN, THEY SAY-- AND THERE I WAS!

"BORN ON CHRISTMAS DAY, AND SHOWERED WITH TOYS FROM MY FATHER WINSLOW EVERY YEAR!

"BUT EVENTUALLY, FATHER STOPPED PAYING ATTENTION TO ME, AND STARTED DOTING ON ALL THE OTHER LITTLE GIRLS AND BOYS. I WAS TOO OLD FOR HIM TO LOVE!

"MOTHER COULDN'T STAND THOSE OTHER CHILDREN, THOUGH, SO SHE TOOK ME AWAY ONE NIGHT WHILE HE WAS OUT PLAYING WITH THOSE BRATS!"

BUT THEN LAST YEAR, MOTHER WENT *AWAY*. LEFT ME ON A STREET CORNER IN DOWNTOWN METROPOLIS.

"I HAD NO OTHER FAMILY. NO HOPE.

"I TRIED TO GO BACK TO FATHER, BUT I ONLY FOUND AN OLD WORKSHOP OF HIS.

"I *LEARNED* FROM HIS THINGS, LEARNED ABOUT THE *LEGACY* I WAS TO UPHOLD.

"THEN I STARTED GATHERING UP SOME *NEW* FRIENDS!

"OTHER BOYS AND GIRLS WHO'D BEEN *ABANDONED* BY THEIR PARENTS!"

AND THEN I FOUND OUT ABOUT *YOU*.

FATHER MADE YOU *SUFFER*. TOOK YOUR SON AWAY FROM YOU.

BUT THERE'S GOOD NEWS! HE'S GIVEN YOU SOMETHING BETTER!

WE CAN FULFILL EACH OTHER'S NEEDS! I NEEDED TO HURT MY FATHER, AND YOU NEED A NEW BABY BOY!

ME!

SO WHAT DO YOU SAY?

WILL YOU BE MY NEW *MOMMY?*

HAVE YOU EVER BEEN ASKED TO **HELP** SOMEONE YOU ABSOLUTELY **DESPISED?**

SOMEONE WHO MAKES YOUR SKIN CRAWL, WHO MAKES YOUR STOMACH **CHURN** WHEN YOU THINK OF THEM?

CAT GRANT--MY **LEAST FAVORITE** DAILY PLANET REPORTER-- CAME TO ME WITH A STORY.

THE FAMILIES OF METROPOLIS WERE UNDER ATTACK.

THIS STARTED AFTER CAT FOUND OUT LANA LANG KNEW ME *PERSONALLY.*

SOMEONE HAD BEEN SENDING CAT MESSAGES IN THE MAIL. *DOLLS.* EACH OF THEM ARRIVING TO COINCIDE WITH THE KIDNAPPING OF A CHILD IN THE CITY.

SHE'D GOTTEN *THREE* OF THEM SO FAR.

CAT NEEDED SUPERMAN'S HELP. KAL WAS *UNAVAILABLE,* THOUGH, SO SHE USED WHAT SHE KNEW ABOUT LANA TO GET ACCESS TO ME.

"THE HERO THE WORLD DOESN'T NEED," CAT ONCE WROTE ABOUT ME.

SOME DAYS, THOUGH, IT SURE FEELS LIKE IT *DOES.*

THOUGH, IF THERE WEREN'T THREE KIDS MISSING, I'M NOT SURE I'D HELP HER.

YOU CAN'T SAY THOSE KINDS OF THINGS ABOUT A PERSON THEN EXPECT THEM TO JUST *FLY UP* AND GIVE YOU A HAND.

CAT'S GOT A HISTORY WITH *TOYMAN,* SO HE WAS OUR FIRST SUSPECT.

WE BROUGHT HIM THE DOLLS. HE SEEMED TO RECOGNIZE THE WORK, BUT THEN ONE SPRANG TO LIFE AND PUT HIM IN CRITICAL CONDITION.

SO WITH NO *ACTIVE LEADS...*

...AFTER BEATING THE 'NOG OUT OF EVERY VILLAIN I COULD FIND, I'M BACK WHERE I STARTED.

LEAD-LESS IN A CITY OF MILLIONS.

I WISH SOMEONE SOMEWHERE KNEW SOMETHING ABOUT THIS GUY. I DON'T FIND HIM, THOSE KIDS WON'T BE HOME FOR CHRISTMAS.

AND I *KNOW* WHAT IT'S LIKE TO MISS YOUR FAMILY ON A HOLIDAY.

"SO."

WHAT *ARE* YOU?

WHAT DO YOU MEAN?

MY SISTER *DIED.* THE SUPERWOMAN SUIT GENERAL LANE CREATED--

"OUR FATHER, WHO ART IN HEAVEN."

--GAVE YOU POWERS. SUPERGIRL DAMAGED IT AND YOU *EXPLODED.* YOU WERE *VAPORIZED.*

THEN YOU CAME *BACK,* WITH ALL OF THE POWERS *INSIDE* YOU. ALIEN D.N.A. GRAFTED ONTO YOURS.

I UNDERSTAND DR. LIGHT IS TRYING TO STRIP THEM OUT OF YOU--

AND DOING SUCH A *SUPER* JOB, ISN'T SHE? SHE'S PULLING THEM OUT STRAND-BY-STRAND, BUT IT'S TAKING A *LOT* OF TIME. TIME WHERE SHE GETS TO WATCH ME *SQUIRM.*

BEFORE YOU GET ANY FURTHER IN YOUR *SUMMARY* OF MY RECENT HISTORY, LOIS, TELL ME...

...WHY *DID* YOU COME HERE? TO WISH ME A HAPPY HOLIDAY?

OR SO WE COULD RAISE A GLASS TO OUR PARENTS? (MAY THEY REST IN *PEACE.*)

NO. I CAME SO I COULD LOOK YOU IN THE *EYE* AND TELL YOU SOMETHING.

AND WHAT IS THAT?

YOU DISGUST ME.

WHAT?

MY SISTER WAS... BRIGHT. NO, *LUMINESCENT.* A WONDERFUL GIRL.

SHE WOULD ALWAYS SMILE, EVEN WHEN THINGS WERE AT THEIR *WORST.* WHEN SHE WAS TEMPORARILY STRUCK BLIND. WHEN THE ONLY JOB SHE COULD GET WAS AS A FLIGHT ATTENDANT.

BUT WHEN DAD DIED, I COULD TELL SHE WAS *CHANGING.* WHEN SHE JOINED THE MILITARY, I THOUGHT IT WAS JUST TO HONOR DAD...

...BUT AT WHAT POINT DID SHE STOP BEING MY SISTER AND BECOME THIS...THIS *MONSTER?*

Stasis Field: Active

I--I WAS GIVEN *ORDERS* BY DAD, LOIS--

WHICH IS A *PITIFUL* EXCUSE! MY SISTER WOULD KNOW THAT.

YOU ALLOWED YOURSELF TO BECOME A KILLING MACHINE TO IMPRESS A MAN WHO DIDN'T EVEN *CARE* ABOUT YOU WHEN WE WERE KIDS--

HE CARED MORE ABOUT *ME* THAN HE DID ABOUT *YOU* AT THE END!

YOU WERE THE ONE WHO WAS ALWAYS RUNNING AWAY TO FOLLOW AN *ALIEN.* YOU WERE SO FOCUSED ON THE MAN OF STEEL, YOU STOPPED CARING FOR YOUR FAMILY.

SO WHO CAN BLAME DAD FOR HOW HE *FELT* ABOUT YOU? HE PICKED ME UP FROM THE *DEPTHS* AND MADE ME INTO SOMETHING *GREATER--*

NO.

GENERAL LANE TOOK ADVANTAGE OF PEOPLE WHO DIDN'T KNOW ANY BETTER BECAUSE OF A STUPID, XENOPHOBIC GRUDGE WHICH TOOK *THOUSANDS* OF LIVES...

...AND WORST OF ALL, HE TOOK YOUR SOUL IN THE PROCESS.

I CAN'T FORGIVE HIM. NOT FOR ANY OF IT. NOR CAN I FORGIVE YOU FOR BEING SO STUPID.

GOODBYE, SUPERWOMAN. I DON'T MISS GENERAL LANE.

BUT I MISS MY SISTER ALREADY.

"WELL?! WHADDAYA *THINK?*"

WILL YOU BE MOTHER TO ME AND MY *AMAZING* DOLL-FRIENDS?!

I KNOW IT MIGHT SEEM OVERWHELMING AT FIRST, BUT I'M REALLY A *WONDERFUL* CHILD. I'LL BE EVEN BETTER THAN THE CHILD MY FATHER TOOK FROM YOU...

MMMMMM, MMFFNNNL!

OH I HOPE THAT'S A "YES, I'LL BE YOUR MOM" MMM MM! WHAT WERE YOU SAYING, MOTHER DEAREST?

HOW COULD YOU *POSSIBLY THINK* YOU COULD EVER REPLACE MY *CHILD*?!

I DON'T KNOW WHAT KIND OF *PSYCHOPATH* YOU ARE, BUT YOU'RE NOT *HALF* THE MAN MY SON WOULD BE IF HE WERE ALIVE TODAY!

I... YOU...

NO, NO, *NO!*

THIS IS TURNING OUT ALL *WRONG!* YOU'RE SUPPOSED TO *APPRECIATE* MY EFFORTS!

YOU'RE SUPPOSED TO LOVE ME LIKE I LOVE *YOU.*

I WOULDN'T LOVE YOU IF YOU WERE THE *LAST CHILD* IN METROPOLIS, YOU LITTLE FREAK.

Y-YOU-- YOU CAN'T STOP ME!

YOU HAVE TO LET ME GO!

FIGURES. LIKE ALL VILLAINS, ONCE YOU'RE LEFT STANDING *ALONE*, YOU'RE BEGGING AND COWARDLY.

YOU TORTURED THREE LITTLE KIDS. WHY SHOULD I LET YOU DO *ANYTHING*?

B-BECAUSE IF YOU *DON'T*, I'LL *KILL* THOSE LITTLE KIDS! MY DOLL-FRIENDS!

EXCUSE ME?

I'VE GOT-- GOT *BOMBS* STRAPPED TO THEIR CHESTS! ONE FLICK OF THIS BUTTON, AND--

AAHHH!

HA! YOU MISSED ME!

SHE WASN'T AIMING FOR *YOU*, YOU LITTLE BASTARD.

215

THIS IS FOR MY *SON!*

KRAK

HE'D BE ABOUT YOUR AGE RIGHT NOW, AND HE'D BE DAMNED *MAGNIFICENT.*

WOW. *T.K.O.*

YES, WELL... WHEN YOU'VE DATED THE MEN *I* HAVE, YOU LEARN TO THROW A PUNCH.

I DON'T... I DON'T REALLY HAVE *TIME* TO DATE.

CAT, WHAT WAS ALL OF THIS *ABOUT?*

THIS IS WINSLOW SCHOTT'S *SON.* HE'S DISTURBED. KEPT GOING ON AND ON ABOUT HOW HE WANTED ME TO BE HIS--

MOM?

C-CAN SOMEONE HELP ME FIND MY *MOM?*

ELI?

IT'S-- IT'S OKAY. WE'RE GOING TO GET YOU OUT OF THIS *SUIT--*

THAT MAN...HE-- HE *HURT* ME...

I KNOW. I KNOW. HE WON'T HURT YOU AGAIN. HE WON'T HURT *ANYONE* AGAIN.

EVERYTHING'S GOING TO BE OKAY.

FROM NOW ON, WE'RE *ALL* GOING TO BE OKAY...

"AND HOW ARE THOSE KIDS NOW?"

217

THE NEXT DAY.

I TALKED TO THE DOCTORS AT METROPOLIS GENERAL.

THE KIDS HAVE BEEN *REUNITED* WITH THEIR PARENTS AND SEEM TO BE DOING OKAY, ALL THINGS CONSIDERED.

THEY'LL DEFINITELY NEED THERAPY, THOUGH.

AND TOYMAN?

STILL IN INTENSIVE CARE, BUT THEY THINK HE'LL PULL THROUGH.

WELL, I'M GLAD YOU WERE THERE FOR *CAT*, KARA. EVEN IF SHE DIDN'T APPEAR TO APPRECIATE THE *SAVE*.

SHE'S BEEN THROUGH A LOT, TOO. WE *ALL* HAVE. SOME OF US JUST FIND DIFFERENT WAYS TO DEAL WITH IT THAN OTHERS.

HEY!

LOOK WHO I FOUND.

MERRY CHRISTMAS, GUYS! CLARK HERE YET?

EXPECTING HIM *SHORTLY*.

DID YOU HEAR ABOUT TOMORROW'S *PLANET* HEADLINE YET, KARA?

NO, WHY?

SNEAK PEEK OF THE *PROOFS*. ONE OF THE ADVANTAGES OF BEING THE EDITOR-IN-CHIEF'S *FAVORITE* REPORTER.

MERRY CHRISTMAS.

WHAT'S IT *SAY?*

WHEN IT COMES DOWN TO IT, LIVES CAN BE BOILED DOWN TO JUST A FEW THINGS:

OUR FAMILIES...

SEE? SHE'S NOT ALL BAD.

NO. NOT *ALL.*

YOUR PARENTS WOULD BE SO *PROUD* OF YOU, KARA. I KNOW *WE* ARE.

...BOTH THE GOOD PARTS...

...AND THE BAD...

...THE PEOPLE WHO HATE US...

...THE ONES WHO *LOVE* US...

...AND THE WORK WE LEAVE *BEHIND.* SOME OF US TRY *HARD* TO MAKE THE WORLD A BETTER PLACE THAN IT WAS WHEN WE FOUND IT.

THANKS, CAT.

I KNOW THAT'S WHAT I TRY TO DO. I KNOW I WON'T *ALWAYS* BE SUCCESSFUL.

BUT THAT'S LIFE.

Gates & Igle spotted in Bahamas! Page A5

DAILY PLANET
THE DAY I NEEDED SUPERGIRL

BY CAT GRANT

Just over a year ago, I wrote about why I believed the world didn't need Supergirl.

I was sick of watching a young girl fly across the skies and do more harm than good. While I stand by the article I wrote at the time, recent events in my personal life have led me to reexamine that statement. While I'm not exactly sure what effect the "Girl of Steel" has on the world, I can tell you that as one of those she helped, there came a day when I needed Supergirl.

What I did not consider in my earlier dismissal of Supergirl was that I was dismissing a work in progress. On one hand, I still don't like her outfit or her attitude (or her errors in the field), but I have come to appreciate her desire to help others.

With three children missing, Supergirl spent Christmas Eve searching for clues to the children's whereabouts. She rescued the children-- and me -- from a criminal nicknamed "The Dollmaker." The Dollmaker had kidnapped me from my home after stalking me for months.

Say what you will about the length of her skirt or the length of her experience, but I've been shown by this ordeal that you cannot be judged simply by those things. All of us make mistakes, even 'Metropolis' greatest heroes.

Those of us who rise above it--or, for that matter, fly--deserve second chances. I'm willing to give Supergirl another chance, and I now ask you, Daily Planet readers, to do the same.

I'M SUPERGIRL

THIS IS MY LIFE...

...AND Y'KNOW WHAT?

continued on B7

I'M PRETTY HAPPY WITH IT.

(FOR NOW, AT LEAST.)

Photo by James Olsen

THE END

SUPERGIRL #58 VARIANT COVER
AMANDA CONNER & PAUL MOUNTS
after CURT SWAN

FROM THE WRITER OF *JUSTICE LEAGUE* & *GREEN LANTERN*

GEOFF JOHNS
with GARY FRANK

SUPERMAN:
THE LAST SON OF
KRYPTON

with RICHARD DONNER &
ADAM KUBERT

SUPERMAN
& THE LEGION OF
SUPER-HEROES

with GARY FRANK

SUPERMAN: BRAINIAC

with GARY FRANK

START AT THE BEGINNING!

SUPERMAN: ACTION COMICS VOLUME 1: SUPERMAN AND THE MEN OF STEEL

SUPERMAN VOLUME 1: WHAT PRICE TOMORROW?

SUPERGIRL VOLUME 1: THE LAST DAUGHTER OF KRYPTON

SUPERBOY VOLUME 1: INCUBATION

*"Clear storytelling at its best. It's an intriguing
concept and easy to grasp."—THE NEW YORK TIMES*

*"Azzarello is rebuilding the mythology of Wonder Woman."
—CRAVE ONLINE*

START AT THE BEGINNING!

WONDER WOMAN
VOLUME 1: BLOOD

WONDER WOMAN
VOL. 2: GUTS

by BRIAN
AZZARELLO and
CLIFF CHIANG

WONDER WOMAN
VOL. 3: IRON

by BRIAN
AZZARELLO and
CLIFF CHIANG

SUPERGIRL VOL. 1:
LAST DAUGHTER OF
KRYPTON

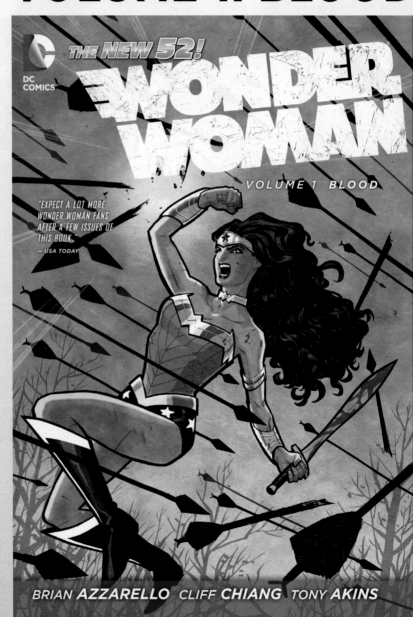

BRIAN **AZZARELLO** CLIFF **CHIANG** TONY **AKINS**